THE LEFT WITHIN THE MALTESE
LABOUR MOVEMENT

THE LEFT
WITHIN THE
MALTESE LABOUR
MOVEMENT

John Chircop

Mireva Publications

First Published in 1991
by Mireva Publications Limited,
(Mireva and Logo are Registered Trade Marks. Reg. No. 17998)
of Tower Street, Msida, Malta.
Typeset and paged on New Century Schoolbook 10/12 pt.
Produced by Evan Cumbo.
Printed by Gutenberg Press,
Zabbar, Malta.

International Standard Book Number

1-870579-10-0

To Jacqueline

Contents

Contents

List of Illustrations

List of Plates

Abbreviations

AMILP	- Anglo-Maltese Independent Labour Party (Branch of the British ILP)
Art.	- Article
Ch.	- Chapter
Des.	- Dispatch
Encl.	- Enclosure (in dispatch)
GHPM	- Ghakda Proletaria Maltija
GHSM	- Ghakda Socialista Maltija
ICWPA	- International Class War Prisoners Aid
ILP	- Independent Labour Party
ILP (B)	- Independent Labour Party (British)
LP	- Labour Party, also Partit tal-Haddiema
MGG	- Malta Goverranent Gazette
MRC	- Malta Royal Commission 1931
PAV	- Palace Archives Valletta
PDN	- Partito Democratico Nazionalista
PN	- Partito Nazionalista (Nationalist Party)
PNM	- Partit Nazionalista Malti
PPM	- Partito Popolare Maltese
Sda	- Strada
SSC	- State Secretary for the Colonies
ST	- Sedition Trial 1933 (Court Archives, Valletta)
Str.	- Street
Tip.	- Tipografia (Printing Press)
UPM	- Unione Politica Maltese

Variations of Names

Agius, Salvu	- S. Agius
Azzopardi, Wigi	- U. Azzopardi
Boffa, Pawlu	- Dr Paul Boffa
	- P. Boffa
Bugeja, Censu	- C. Bugeja
	- V. Bugeja
Chetcuti, Francesco	- F. Chetcuti
Chetcuti, Martin	- M. Chetcuti
Degiorgio, Duminku	- D. Degiorgio
Delicata, Salvu	- S. Delicata
	- Saver Delicata
Ellul, Guzè	- Guzè Ellul (Mercer)
	- Giusè Ellul
	- G. Ellul (Mercer)
Gatt, Gianni	- G. Gatt
Grech, Joseph	- J. Grech
Mamo, Juann	- J. Mamo
Marks, John F.,	- John Francis Marks
	- J. F. Marks
	- J.F.M.
Mizzi, Enrico	- E. Mizzi
Orlando, Guzè	- Giusè Orlando Smith
	- G. Orlando
	- Joseph Orlando Smith
Pace, Joseph	- J. Pace
Pulis, Salvu	- S. Pulis
Valvo, Ganni	- John Valvo
	- J. Valvo
Zammit, Salvu	- S. Zammit

Foreword

To someone familiar with the contemporary Maltese political scene, dominated as it is by two parties, one of which is Christian Democrat and the other pragmatic Socialist in outlook, it is surprising, if not incredible, that in much less enlightened times than we claim to live in today there could have existed in Malta a radical left-wing movement as the one discussed in this work. The perseverance of these radicals, which found them friendless when the final clamp-down came in 1933, would seem quixotic but for the fact that many, though not all, of their views and ideals are today accepted as a matter of course. For, in the 1920s, compromise and caution seemed the only safe course for anyone left of centre in politics. Self-government, the context within which the nascent Labour movement sought to improve the lot of the working class, in practice required politicians to keep in mind always that at the end of the day nothing could be achieved without the sanction of the two real powers in Malta: the British administration and the Roman Catholic Church.

It is not difficult to understand how a people, who has been controlled by one outsider or other ever since it can record, should find it hard to identify its own interests with those of its rulers. Such alienation inevitably brings forth leaders from within the community, leaders who in due course acquire formidable power over the lives of the people they lead. Like the Poles or the Irish, the Maltese entrusted their spiritual pastors with their social and political leadership. During the last phase of Malta's colonial history the British were quite content to sanction and even encourage, within certain limitations, the leadership role of the Roman Catholic clergy in Maltese society. Because they were in Malta for its strategic value, security considerations required a disciplined population whose loyalty was beyond question. Sound political common sense therefore disposed the British to strike a special relationship with the powerful spiritual leaders of the Maltese, a relationship that was tantamount to sharing power.

For a long time this relationship enabled the British to ignore largely the persistent demands of Maltese secular leaders for a significant role in the government of the internal affairs of Malta. This, despite the forceful argument that it was the Maltese who had invited themselves into the British Empire. As the nineteenth century progressed, the spread of liberalism in Europe and the perseverance of a section of the Maltese middle class in demanding responsible government led the British to experiment with conceding varying doses of participation in the internal government of Malta. This coincided with a growing conviction among British administrators that English culture should be diffused more seriously among the Maltese population. The campaign of the emerging political class for a greater share in government therefore compounded with their resistance to what they regarded as the cultural colonization of Malta. As a result the political scene of the last decades of the nineteenth century was dominated by the struggle between the English and Italian languages waged within the framework of a representative constitution. In reaction to the middle-class, predominantly pro-Italian, politicians, mostly drawn from the legal profession, emerged the pro-British political movement, which drew support from, among others, the disenfranchised industrial working class.

For the British were not just the administrators of Malta: they were also the biggest employers providing thousands of jobs in the service establishments, notably the Admiralty dockyard. For these workers the acrimonious debate over Italian and English was largely inconsequential they could speak or read neither except in so far as it continued to suffocate the chances of their children's education. But between the 'Italian' and 'English' political movements they perceived that the latter was slightly more conscious of their social needs than the former. More importantly perhaps, they generally were not given to biting the hand that fed them, however irregularly. The novelty of Manuel Dimech and the ideas he stood for lay in that he was the first to break, or at least crack, the cast of opportunism among this industrial working class. By identifying and exposing the actors that wielded power in Malta, he defined the basic socialist principle that the working class ultimately stood alone and must fight its own struggle. Because he attacked at once the British, the Church, the wealthy, and the politicians, he was of course cut down by all these together. But it is no coincidence that both serious trade-unionism and, subsequently, the backbone of the Labour Party emerged from the same dockyard where Dimechianism had been bred.

The first generation organizers and leaders of the Labour Party were on the whole a more cautious and pragmatic set of socialists than the Dimechian pioneers. Operating within the framework of the self-government constitution and a broader, though not universal, franchise, they were by no means radical and limited their programme to modest but attainable social measures. Their political strategy was to avoid confrontation where possible with the British authorities, the Church, or even the other political parties and indeed offer their cooperation where this might facilitate the fulfilment of the Labour programme. The Compact between the Labour Party and the pro-British Constitutional Party was the culmination of this strategy. In some ways the political circumstances of the late 1920s still had not changed much from those of the 1890s. Yet it is ironic that the Labour Party, compromise and caution notwithstanding, should have had to endure the same kind of damnation as Dimech himself, not for being radical, but for being allied to the Constitutionals. This in itself is an indication of how much the radicals described in this work were ahead of their times, if not of our times.

Dr Dominic Fenech

Preface

Little research has been carried out so far on the historical development of the Labour movement in these islands. This lacuna is much more evident in the historiography of the left in the workers' movement. The main reason for this is probably the scarcity of primary documentation. In fact, this was the first challenge in embarking on this book. Pamphlets, tracts, flysheets, journals, and other printed matter published by leftist organizations or other radical elements have been traced and found in different places, especially in the possession of surviving protagonists. Important material has unfortunately been lost, and most of the documentation, correspondence, and agitprop were destroyed for fear of trouble with the police, especially in the wake of the 1933 sedition raids. An urgent need is felt for extant material to be rescued and made available for students of this period.

An important consideration about this study must be pointed out. Even if the title of this book may suggest a comprehensive study which encompasses this field in every aspect, it must be clearly stated that its objective is to arouse interest in this particular area of research which has for too long been neglected.

Invaluable source material was provided by oral testimonies which were instrumental for research, especially where important references and suggestions were offered. They have also given the author an important human experience and a deep sense of historical empathy.

I would therefore like to thank the various people who, with patience, agreed to be interviewed or who gave me important information in various forms. My heartfelt thanks go to Carmelo Carabott, Tom Ritchie, Carmelo Zammit, and others who do not wish to be named.

Another most important source has been the Sedition Case Trial of 1933, the record of which is deposited in the Law Courts Archives at Valletta. As I was the first person to be given permission to see these stenographed proceedings, thanks must go to those who helped me obtain this special permission.

Last, but not least, a heartfelt thanks goes to Dr Dominic Fenech for his suggestions, an for the time he spent discussing this work with me. I must also thank Professor Godfrey Wettinger, for his generous suggestions and his comments on the first draft of the manuscript.

John Chircop

1

The 1921 Constitution and its Aftermath

On 30 April 1921 the Letters Patent of a new constitution were promulgated by the Governor, Field-Marshal Viscount Plumer. For Malta — a fortress island colony in the Mediterranean — this constitution signified an important step in the process of state formation. It was the result of two years of drafting, and was to come into effect on 16 May. The general framework of the constitution was a diarchy, with a bicameral legislature taking care of domestic and imperial matters.[1] The legislature was composed of a legislative assembly and a senate.

The Senate had seventeen members. Ten of them were termed 'special members'. The clergy, the university, the Chamber of Commerce, the nobility and the Trade Union Council each nominated two members. The remaining seven were elected by a general electorate entitled to vote according to property qualifications.[2] Therefore, the senate was an institution where

---

[1] A.V. Laferla, *British Malta*, 233.
[2] 'The Malta Constitution 1921', Appendix, *[M]alta [R]oyal [C]ommission 1931, Minutes of Evidence.*

the Maltese traditional clerico-professional and landowning classes held overwhelming power. Not surprisingly it was to be the target of continuous and unabated criticism by working-class intellectuals who saw in it the perpetuation of despotism and control by the traditional conservative ruling classes over the lower classes.[3]

The legislative assembly, consisting of thirty-two elected members, was elected on the principle of proportional representation. Voting was restricted to males over twenty-one years of age, again on the bases of literacy and property qualifications.[4]

In granting constitutions to the Maltese, the British authorities always made sure that this in no way interfered with the latter's security interests. The essential feature of the new constitution was 'that the experiment of entrusting (the Maltese) with that responsibility should not be allowed to endanger the position of Malta as a vital element in our defence'.[5]

According to the colonial authorities, the most expedient formula was that which had been already experimented in India by the Montagu-Chelmsford reforms. This meant a complete division of power between the Imperial security interest and a Maltese government that was to be responsible for domestic issues.[6] The basic principle underlying the granting of self-government lay in this division of power: a principle which, according to the colonial authorities, offered a solution to the impending social and economic crises facing the colony 'in which it was possible to temper recognition for self-government with the safeguarding of wider Imperial interest'.[7] This wider 'imperial interest' had changed as a result of the victory over Germany, but Malta's importance did not diminish and 'with the dissipation of the German naval menace and with the revival of the Eastern problem in a new form, the importance of Malta

---

[3] U. Azzopardi, 'L'Autonomija f'Malta', *Labour Opinion,* 6 December 1923.
[4] 'The Malta Constitution 1921', Appendix, *MRC 1931.*
[5] L.C. Amery, *My Political Life,* vol.2, 194.
[6] *Ibid.*
[7] [P]alace [A]rchives, [V]alletta, Dispatches from Lord Passfield, Secretary for the Colonies, to Governor John Du Cane, 14 January 1931.

in our scheme of defence is certain to increase'.[8] In fact, the main interest of the British in the islands had never been resource-extracting. The only resource of these islands was cheap and reliable labour for the Admiralty docks and the other Services. The main British interest in Malta was its geostrategic location in the Mediterranean. This is borne out by the Colonial Office conception of the Maltese as 'living on the outskirts of a British fortress and providing cheap labour for a British dockyard.'[9]

With the diarchy system of governing, 'reserved matters', including security and foreign relations, remained in the hands of the imperial side of government. Once the ready supply of labour was guaranteed the British were more than prepared to leave the local traditional middle classes and the Catholic Church alone, to maintain and enjoy their social hegemony.

The *Assemblea Nazionale*, largely representing the Maltese élite, which had assembled in 1919 to agitate for a new constitution, had been consulted and had worked together with the Colonial Office in the drafting of the new constitution. It was clear that the local Assembly would find a *modus vivendi* on the general lines of a self-governing constitution, if the interests it represented were guaranteed. The Colonial Office accepted much of the Assembly's draft constitution which was made out in the framework of a 'diarchy'. The Assembly accepted the principle that 'reserved matters' would stay under the jurisdiction of the colonial authorities.[10] This 1921 constitution therefore was created by mutual consent between the colonial authorities and the *Assemblea Nazionale*. Thus, even though one of the main factors that had led to the granting of self-government was the 1919 riots, where the physical vanguard were the working masses,[11] it was the privileged classes which gained power, albeit restricted.

---

[8] Amery, 194-195.
[9] Amery, 195.
[10] H. Ganado, *Rajt Malta Tinbidel*, 237.
[11] Ċ. Bugeja, 'Is-sebgħa ta' Ġunju – il-bidu tal-Ħelsien', *Il Ħmar*, 9 June 1928.

While the new constitution represented a power-sharing arrangement between the British authorities and the Maltese ruling classes, once it came into operation the strife between the working classes and the privileged classes surfaced. The latter according to Dr Paul Boffa, who became leader of the Labour Party,

'continued to thrive on the tradition established during the rule of the knights *[Knights of Malta, Order of St John]*throughout the period of British rule until the war, when the question of self-government was seriously mottled. But the dominant class desired self-government only in so far as they could obtain a Constitution which would perpetuate their domination over the masses.'[12]

This noticeable use of the masses by the local ruling classes to further their own interests, in fact, contributed considerably to the political polarization of society.[13]

The working masses were never represented or consulted on the matter, as their representation in the *Assemblea Nazionale* was minimal. Furthermore all discussions and proceedings were conducted in Italian, a language very few working people understood. Paradoxically this political ignorance in itself enabled the Assembly to feign that it represented all classes.[14]

Having gained self-government, the local dominant classes never stepped beyond their limits of jurisdiction. In the first four years, at least, these classes were content to have their control over domestic affairs assured, leaving the British satisfied that 'the fluctuations of internal politics have not interfered with the issues which matter from the point of view of Imperial security'.[15]

[12] *MRC 1931*, evidence of Dr P. Boffa, 60.
[13] Ċ. Bugeja, 'Is-sebgħa ta' Ġunju': *'fil cliċca dominanti u fil cotra miċhuda issehem li jistħokkilha fil ħajja nazzjonali ta Malta'* [in the dominant clique and in the masses denied their rightful share in Malta's national life.]
[14] *MRC 1931*, 60-61.
[15] Amery, 196.

Boffa reasoned that as long as 'the Constitution fulfilled the function of a fortress against the assault of real democracy, it was said that it worked well. That was in the first six years of self-government.'[16] Similarly, the left-wing intellectual Ċensu Bugeja concluded that the contingent opportunity which self-government gave all classes to unite and to begin evolving into a nation were frustrated by the abuse of power by, and in the interests of, the dominant classes.[17]

Also in opposition to the traditional ruling parties was the veteran politician Gerald Strickland, the leader of the Constitutional Party. Strickland had never been able to see eye to eye with the clerico-professional politicians, whom he regarded as disloyal. In the 1920s, British dispatches and the colonial officials in general thought of Strickland as 'a man of old English and Maltese stock, sincerely pro-British but singularly misguided in all his actions'.[18] Strickland had a missionary view of the British Empire. He believed that Imperial interests and the interests of the Maltese people were intertwined and were obstructed only by the pro-Italian middle-classes. Strickland was seen as the politician who could obstruct the 1921 constitution arrangement because of his anti-Italianization policies, even though he was regarded as the Empire's stooge in Malta. He also led a party which represented a new emerging middle-class, and who worked against any compromise between the pro-Italian clerico-professional classes and the Imperial authorities.

This is yet another reason why the pro-Italian élite, and especially the Church, was more prepared to compromise on certain issues with the Imperial side of government than with Strickland during the first years of the constitution. This was before pro-Italian irredentist tendencies became pronounced and came to be seen as a threat to the security of the island within

---

[16] *MRC 1931*, 60.
[17] A Nation, according to Ċensu Bugeja, meant *'a true Nation, fully fledged — a people organised in a union by their common language, customs, traditions, and helping each other in progress'*. 'Malta Nazion', *Il Hmar*, 5 October 1927).
[18] R. Viscount Swinton, *I Remember*, 89.

the British Imperial framework. Later, in 1933, under a Nationalist government, this situation was to become so alarming
that the Colonial authorities resorted to direct colonial rule, on
the grounds that the 1921 constitutional compromise had been
broken by the Maltese counterpart, a measure which the Nationalists called, significantly, a *coup d'état*.[19]

The Roman Catholic Church in Malta as part of the local traditional ruling classes, was also party to the compromise of the
1921 constitution. Self-government came as a relief for the local
Church because it signified the end of any attempt by the British
at protestantizing the Maltese. The British always tried to be
on good terms with the local church in the interests of their
security, because the church was the only popular institution
which could guarantee the people's loyalty. In compensation,
the church had been exempted from taxation,[20] and granted
other privileges. The power of the church was virtually un-
contested, and it had a strong base in the senate. On many issues
it aligned itself with the professional classes against anything
which smelt of reformism.

The 1921 constitution did not state that the official religion
of Malta was Roman Catholic, but granted liberty of conscience
and religious worship, despite the declaration draft of the
Assemblea. But in his dispatch of 9 April, covering the Letters
Patent, the Secretary of State suggested that the above declaration draft should be laid down, read and approved in the first
meeting of the National Legislature.[21] This was considered to
be 'a splendid compromise worthy of the best English traditions
and satisfactory even to the ecclesiastical authorities'.[22] So the
Catholic hierarchy had once again secured its own interests and
its hegemony over the people by a compromise with the colonial
authorities. A similar compromise had been reached by the

---

[19] Anon., *La questione nazionale e linguistica dopo il colpo di stato del 2
Novembre 1933*.
[20] D. Fenech, *The making of Archbishop Gonzi*, 6.
[21] Ganado, 239.
[22] Laferla, 234.

Church, the state and Maltese dominant classes in their battle against Manwel Dimech (1860 — 1921). Dimech had become their common enemy. His charisma had held together a political grouping composed of the best class-conscious elements of the urban lower classes. These, later to become known by their leader's surname (Dimechiani), began to influence the working class in a secularist socialistically-oriented way.

Thus Manwel Dimech championed the cause of the working classes and the oppressed. He was the exponent of a radical ideology; an amalgamation of revolutionary jacobinism, classical nationalism, and anti-colonialism with a heavy socialist imprint. He thought of overthrowing the British authorities and forming a Maltese Republic, ideas which were propagated in his own journal *Il Bandiera tal Maltin*. With these considerations in mind, Dimech founded the Society of the Enlightened (*Xirca tal Imdaulin*), which name was later changed to Maltese Society (*Xirca Maltia*)[23] which had as its ultimate end the liberation of the Maltese people from colonial oppression. In 1911 Archbishop Pietru Pace excommunicated Dimech. His newspaper *Il Bandiera tal Maltin*, as well as his organization, were also censured on the grounds of being illuminist. Later, prior to the First World War, Dimech was exiled to Egypt, where he died in 1921.[24]

Some of Dimech's followers (*Dimechiani*) together with other elements from different political tendencies, were to become the radical dynamic section behind a network of the first trade unions and working-class organizations which sprang up, mainly from the dockyard.[25]

In Malta, as in Great Britain, trade-unionism gave birth to the Labour Party. This was mostly the case with the dockyard unions, 'first the Imperial Government Workers Union, and subsequently the three local branches that were affiliated to the

---

[23] H. Frendo, *Party Politics in a Fortress Colony : The Maltese Experience*, 148.
[24] Frendo, 150-151.
[25] S. Agius, 'Tagħlim', *L'Unioni Maltija*, 8 February 1919.

British Workers Union.'[26] Matthew Giles, a delegate from the British Workers Union, had been sent to Malta[27] in order to organize the Maltese workers in branches. Branch Number 3, affiliated with some professionals in the *Camera del Lavoro*.[28]

The original founding members of the *Camera del Lavoro* were twelve.[29] With the knowledge that some sort of representative government was in store in 1921, the *Camera* proceeded to form a party by which the workers would be represented in the legislative assembly. Local band clubs and other popular organisations were invited to send delegates to form a general committee for the new party. The first meeting of the general committee was attended by delegates from thirty-one organizations. It was held on 15 March 1921 on the thirtieth anniversary of Pope Leo XIII's issuing of the *Rerum Novarum*,[30] the social encyclical which inspired many of the founders of the *Camera*. From this meeting onwards, the new party began to be seriously organized and was later to be called *Partit tal-Ħaddiema* or *Labour Party*.

The working class, made up mostly of illiterate people, and only just beginning to be organized along party lines, was not represented in the 1921 constitutional compromise. The working masses depended for their living mainly on the British military services, and many of them were, 'attached alike by loyalty and self-interest' to the British empire which they had no desire at all to leave.[31] On the other hand, the majority of them were fervent Catholics and respected the local clerical hierarchy and the professional classes.

---

[26] Frendo, 185.

[27] PAV, (Dispatches from Winston) Churchill, (Secretary for the Colonies,) to (Governor) Plumer, 22 June 1921.

[28] Frendo, 185.

[29] The twelve founding members of the *Camera del Lavoro* were: Anton Agius, William Arena, Ġanni Benċini, Robert Benċini, Carmelo Bonello, Gejtano Bonello, Michel Borg, Mikielanġ Borg, Agostino Matrenza, Anton Schembri, Giaċinto Tua, and Salvu Żammit Hammet. (G. Bonnici, *L-Istorja tal-Partit tal-Ħaddiema*, 27).

[30] Bonnici, 33.

[31] Swinton, 88-89.

A compromise, such as that reached with the granting of the 1921 constitution, had to leave the working classes out, even though they were the ones who had fought and died in the 1919 riots which were one main cause for the granting of the constitution.[32] Riots had broken out on 7 June 1919 on the same day that the *Assemblea Nazionale* had called a meeting in Valletta. The masses entered the city and rioting commenced when stones were thrown at some establishments which had hoisted the Union Jack. The Public Library, the Lyceum, and the offices of the pro-British newspaper *Daily Malta Chronicle*, were attacked and ransacked. The houses of known bourgeois individuals such as that of Colonel Francia, a wheat importer and president of the *Camera del Commercio*, Cassar Torregiani, and Francesco Azzopardi were broken into. During the two days of rioting, four Maltese were killed.[33] Flour mills were looted[34] and other establishments connected with the colonial administration and local business monopolies were ransacked.

The participation of the workers, especially the role of the dockyard proletarians, was important.[35] At the time they were faced with massive discharges. The dockyard workers in fact took a leading part in the riots and only returned to work on 10 June when things had calmed down after the funerals of the patriots.[36]

For these workers, the riots, which ended in tragedy, were intended as protests against the miserable standard of living which they had to endure during and after the Great War. L.C. Amery, later Secretary of State for the Colonies, himself, was to declare that the dockyard workers 'were scandalously underpaid. During the war they had subsisted on overtime and on the surplus

---

[32] Bugeja, 'Is-sebgħa ta' Ġunju'.
[33] Ġ. Azzopardi, *Meta il-Malti għadab, is-7 ta' Ġunju 1919 − 60 sena wara*, 17-23 : The four Maltese killed were Carmelo Abela, Emmanuel Attard, Giuseppe Bajada, and Lorenzo Dyer.
[34] Ġ. Azzopardi, 35.
[35] P. Bartolo, *X'kien ġara sew fis-Sette Giugno*, 48-55.
[36] R. Borg, The Maltese Worker 1919-1939, 9.

food and clothing thrown away by the hospitals; and this was one of the main reasons for the riot.'[37] Any concessions to the emerging working classes would have meant change in the economic, social, and political order of things: change which the local dominant classes could not tolerate. As no material improvement was produced by this constitution, the poor remained poor, hungry, and illiterate. In the interwar years, the workers were still paying seven per cent of the national revenue in tax on wheat. When this, together with property contribution to the national budget, were discussed in 1918, there was a great outcry by lawyers, merchants, the Cathedral Chapter, and the Archbishop.[38]

So, the workers were completely left out from this compromise, and this was easily perceived by radical elements, such as the Dimechian Juann Mamo who wrote that this constitution meant nothing new to the toiling masses. Accordingly, the ones who gained were those few who took part in the compromise and gained more direct political and economic power.[39]

Another clear sign of this temporary compromise between the Imperial authorities and the local ruling classes represented in the *Assemblea*, was the adoption of the *pari passu* system concerning the language question. The latter was the manifestation of deeply rooted historical, economic, and social struggles in the cultural superstructure. Italian was the cultural language

---

[37] Amery, 193.

[38] R. Borg, *The Maltese Worker 1919-1939*, 4.

[39] Juann Mamo wrote 'Ftit u ftit uisk, li tista tghoddhom fuk subghajc, jistghu icantau l-Innu tal-Autonomija, li din b'li maghha ġiebet huma, minn minestra f'nofs in nhar u ġbejna friska fil ghaxija ta cull jum il lum keghdin jeclu ir-raviul, u jixorbu il birra ta Ind. Coop. u ikarmċiu il kubbajt ta Żerrek. Mill bkija f'sentejn Autonomija x'hadna tal-minestra misjura bil ġdur xerfin? X'ha il pajjis?' [Few, precious few, indeed perhaps less than ten, can sing the Hymn to Autonomy, which resulted in their dining daily on ravioli washed down with Ind. Coop's beer and Zerrek's nougat for dessert, when formerly it was just vegetable soup for lunch and fresh cheese for supper. As for the rest of us, during two years of Autonomy, what did we get in return for vegetable soup made with hard turnips? What did the country get out of it?] (J. Mamo, 'X'jehtieġ il Malti biex jistehja', *Il Fkir Malti,* 4 October 1923).

of the local traditional élite, whose mode of expression and aspirations were pro-Italian and Catholic. In fact according to section 57 of this new constitution, Italian and English were to be considered the two cultural and official languages in Malta. The Maltese language, the means of communication of the common people, was left only to be used as an instrument for teaching the lower elementary classes. Speeches in the legislative assembly were to be officially published in English or Italian, even if a few chose to speak in Maltese.[40] This was the act which symbolically exhibited the exclusion from this compromise of all the lower classes of society. It simply sealed the agreement between the ruling forces, which divided power according to their interests in a diarchical system and propagated the continuation of their rule and hegemony over society.

---

[40] Laferla, 236.

MALTESE POPULAR PARTY

ELECTORAL PROGRAMME

AND APPEAL.

Electors of Malta and Gozo,

The present hour is important from a political point of view, for the future as well as for the present life of Malta. After a century of just popular remonstrances the Imperial Government has at last recognised our sacred and indestructible right to govern ourselves.

A duty now devolves upon us: that of showing the Imperial Government that we are ripe for local administration and capable of achieving it. All will depend on the choice you will make of the people who are to represent you in Parliament. None but those persons on whose honesty and whose past there is no doubt, deserve to be trusted. Give your vote to those who before your conscience stand unblemished.

Although the institution of Responsible Government is not a new thing for these Islands, we start now as if on a new regime after over a century in which the Government of these Islands was not a Government by the Maltese People.

We the undersigned, the Candidates of the Maltese Popular Party, sustained by the Maltese Political Union, come before you to ask for your vote.

First of all our Party, and we in its name, consistently with the Declaration of Rights made by the members of the Congress of the 16th June 1802, declare that the people of these Islands are proud of being numbered among the free peoples that form the British Empire. This should suffice to reject, were it necessary, any malicious insinuation which may have ever been made against the loyalty of the Maltese and of our Party.

We pledge ourselves to work, if elected, and indefatigably cooperate to achieve the following:

To conform the whole of our activities in Parliament to the principles of Our Holy Religion; to respect and safeguard the rights of the Church, and to make at the beginning of the first Legislature a solemn declaration by Act of Parliament to the effect that the Roman Apostolic Catholic Religion is, as it had always been in the past, the Religion of these Islands.

To maintain and promote the best spirit of cordiality with the Imperial Government, jealously guarding all our rights, and, moreover, to keep up the best relations with the Military and Naval Authorities.

Any promise of vast radical reforms before one can establish how far the economic condition of these Islands can allow it, would be dangerous and useless. Our duty, however, would be that of carefully studying every means of furthering the economic and moral welfare of these Islands.

We will endorse any good proposal either coming from the Labour Party or

spontaneously prompted by the need of protecting the interests of the proletariat, for we recognize the evident necessity of improving the social and economic condition of the worker. So that with these ends in view we will think out all the factors for the solution of the serious problem of unemployment.

We, therefore, in the name of our Party pledge ourselves to study and carry out useful works that will give employment.

We will take care to legislate for the protection of workmen against sweating and for their compensation and their insurance against misfortunes.

We will promote educational institutions conducive to the moral intellectual and economic improvement of workmen, with special regard to technical instruction sufficient to put them in a position to succeed in competition for employment with foreigners both at home and abroad.

Recognising that compulsory education, if controlled by the Church, will be advantageous to the Island, we undertake to promote it.

We will also try to secure for workmen and for the poor the extension of Charitable institutions.

With regard to the language question:

As a long experience has proved that it has always been easy for the Maltese to study simultaneously even more than two languages (contrary to what somebody wishes to insinuate for unavowable ends, viz. that the Maltese can learn only one language at a time) we promise to adopt the part passu system for the teaching of English and Italian both being useful and necessary. Nevertheless, we will introduce special classes to give ever increasing efficiency and special improvement in a particular language in preference to another for those who might wish to emigrate or to take up a trade career or find employment requiring a better knowledge of that language.

In order to elevate the character and the efficiency of the nation and to promote the moral and material welfare of the Maltese we will adopt the necessary measures for the improvement of the courses of study, encouraging the efficiency of the teaching staff of the Elementary Schools offering them adequate wages. We will try to raise the standard of education, and the study of local history and civilisation on the part of students will receive our attention.

The Maltese Popular Party recognises the need of new institutions and practical reforms to be effected gradually. We will, therefore, set up such economic institutions and adopt such technical methods as might lead to the further development of Agriculture.

We will study the means for the utilization of waste land.

We will enter into agreements with the Military Authorities for the restitution of buildings and sites no longer necessary from a strategic point of view and will try to restrict the zone subject to Military clearance rights so as to help and promote the building industry.

We will encourage to the utmost of our power the creation and development of local industries. The tourist industry will receive our support because we hold that Malta on account of its geographic position in the Mediterranean could and should become a great centre of attraction of foreigners.

We will try gradually to improve our harbour and to render it second to none of the principal ports in the Mediterranean so as to make it of easier and more frequent access.

To be in a position to carry out the projects contemplated by the Maltese Popular Party it will be necessary to reorganise the various departments of the Public Service on the basis of a rational economy in the general administration of the Islands — without any prejudice to the vested rights of the actual members of the Civil Service.

We intend readjusting the system of taxation according to the principle of a fair incidence in proportion to the means of the tax-payer, and will simplify the formalities for the collection of taxes.

With regard to the remuneration of Ministers, Senators and Members of the Legislative Assembly, we recognise in principle the expediency of giving adequate compensation to all, for otherwise such responsible positions would seem reserved for a particular financially privileged class to the exclusion of those, who though well qualified, happen to be in want of financial means. To establish the quantum of such remuneration will be the task of the Assembly.

ELECTORS

This is in brief our Electoral Programme.

It will be easy for you to see that we are making no promise which is not capable of actual, although gradual, fulfilment. Our honesty of purpose makes us avoid any promises which might only be meant to elicit the votes of the various classes of the population.

We appeal to your sound judgement, and, asking you for your vote, we promise, with the help of God, to carry out conscientiously our programme in its entirety.

If you wish us to do so it rests solely with you to resolve to give us your support.

The Candidates of the Maltese Popular Party.

The *Maltese Popular Party* Electoral Manifesto of 1921

2

The Realignment of Forces

THE RIGHT: Clerical dominance in the Labour Party.

A number of the founders and leaders of the Labour Party (Partit tal-Ħaddiema) in Malta tended to be drawn from Catholic-populist quarters. Ġanni Bencini, a landowner and philanthropist, had been an active member of the *Comitato Patriottico* and the editor of its organ, *Voce del Popolo*.[1] He was one of the founders of the *Camera dell'Lavoro* and later of the Labour party. Mikielanġ Borg had also been active in these quarters in his youth. However, he was later held to be a dangerous individual by the Colonial Office[2] as he became politically active on the left, inspired by Dimechianism and socialism. Another well-known philanthropist was Alfons Maria Galea, a most popular and prolific writer in Maltese. He was later to become a prominent Labour senator.

---

[1] The *Comitato Patriottico* was created in 1911 with Mgr. Panzavecchia holding the presidency. One of its functions was to nominate Nationalist candidates for local elections. Frendo, 143, 185.
[2] PAV, Churchill to Plumer, 17 May 1921.

Ġanni Bencini and Alfons Maria Galea formed part of a small nucleus of fervent Catholics who advocated social legislation in favour of the working classes along the lines of Catholic virtues and values. Their emphasis was not on social rights, individual responsibility, and class consciousness, but on charity and humble submissiveness. This view was diametrically opposed to that of the secular, democratic, and progressively-minded minority in the same party.[3]

The Catholic Church had tried to absorb the emerging working-class organizations from the start. It had criticized unions and workers' societies for adopting secular names which had to be changed to Catholic ones.[4] On 26 February 1921, the Unione Cattolica San Giuseppe presented a plan for a project for a confederation of all workers' societies and the political Labour Party. However, some societies did not accept this invitation and the attempt was a complete failure.[5]

Members of the clergy joined the Labour Party to help the other Catholic elements already present secure the Church's influence on the party's policies.[6] The two most prominent clerics in the party's directorship at this time were Canon Carmelo Bugelli and Mgr. Professor Michael Gonzi. Years later, the latter recalled how the party was then full of good Catholics.[7] In 1922, Mgr. Gonzi together with Alfons Maria Galea were elected members of the senate for the Labour Party[8]. Gonzi, who was later to become archbishop of Malta, claimed that he was not interested in politics at the time, but, having been approached to join the party, he had asked Archbishop Dom Maurus Caruana for his advice, whereupon 'the Archbishop ordered him to enlist so that there would be a member of the clergy on the committee'.[9]

---

[3] Ġ. Bencini, Il-Hsieb Taghna', Labour Opinion, 12 October 1922.
[4] Bonnici, 19.
[5] Borg, 202.
[6] Ganado, 244.
[7] F. Previ, 'Il-Moviment Soċjali Nisrani f'hidmet il-Unions u f'oqsma politiċi', It-Torċa, 25 October 1981.
[8] Ganado, 250.
[9] A. Koster, Prelates and Politicians in Malta, 88.

The Catholic Church was apprehensive of the leftist elements in the Labour movement, and mostly of the *Dimechians*. The Church élite regarded some Labour Party personalities such as George Ernest Geoghegan,[10] Joseph Hamilton, William Savona, and Mikielang Borg as either revolutionary (or Dimechian in outlook), liberal-Protestant, or anti-clerical. In their minds no distinction was made between these labels and all were variants of the same accusation: anti-Catholicism. The Church's move to organize the working class under its direct control failed and the next move was to fill the party with its own trusted elements. The Labour Party began to be dominated by professional and clerical elements. The first paragraphs of the first two electoral programmes of the party reflected the chief aims of this preponderant clerical wing.[11]

Through the election of Mgr. Michael Gonzi and Alfons Maria Galea to the senate it was to be expected that an understanding would be reached with the members of the other parties on the right of the political spectrum. Furthermore to combat the radical elements, whether liberal, democratic or socialist, the Maltese archbishop requested Cardinal Bourne, the archbishop of Westminster, to send over a priest qualified to combat socialistic tendencies.[12]

Father Dominic Plater S.J., the founder of the Catholic Women's League and by then a sick man, was sent to Malta in January 1921.[13] He associated himself with Maltese priests from the *Curia* and prominent clerical members of the Labour Party. Plater preached to the workers in accordance with the teachings of the *Rerum Novarum* encyclical. On his first public

---

[10] E. Geoghegan, a prominent personality in the Labour Party in the twenties and thirties, was a propagator of the land tax theory originated by Henry George. This led him into polemics with leading Church personalities such as P. Paris O.P. See series of articles by Anon., 'Il Proprieta Privata', *Militia Christi*, 26 March 1933.

[11] *Il Programm Elettorali tal Partit tal Haddiem*, Malta, 1921.

[12] PAV, Churchill to Plumer, 22 June 1921.

[13] Koster, 87.

appearance in Senglea, he attracted an audience of some 600 workers.[14] This charismatic Jesuit also prepared the foundations of a Catholic organization named *Unione Leoniana.*[15]

Father Plater left a very strong impression among the workers and strengthened the basis of the clerical section in the Labour leadership. His preaching on the *Rerum Novarum* also greatly influenced the ideological stand of this wing[16] which began developing a corporatist type of catholic populism. This encyclical was to be translated into Maltese many times in the first three decades of this century.[17] The influence of *Rerum Novarum* was such that the Labour Party continued celebrating the anniversary of its issue with significant ceremonies.[18]

Even left-wingers had to accept the encyclical as the official party teaching, although they gave it a more radical interpretation. Whereas this grouping emphasized what the encyclical said about the rights of the workers, the clerical wing stressed more the necessity of good relations between Labour and Capital, concentrating on that part of the encyclical which called attention to the workers' duties to their employers.[19] *Rerum Novarum,* written in 1891 by Pope Leo XIII, was considered to be an historical appeal to Catholics to undercut the appeal of Socialism by taking the initiative in the fight against bad living and working conditions.'[20]

The Church's manoeuvering with the right clerical wing in the Labour Party was part of a much greater movement which was developing into a conservative block. The latter consisted of the traditional ruling classes and their representatives in the

---

[14] *Ibid.*
[15] PAV, Churchill to Plumer, 22 June 1921.
[16] Militia Christi, April 1931.
[17] P.F. Bellanti, *Enciclica Rerum Novarum*, 1921. Also P. Paris O.P., *Rerum Novarum fuk il condizionijiet tan nies tax xoghol*, 1930.
[18] Laburista, 'Ir Rerum Novarum', *Il Hmara*, 21 May 1930.
[19] For a comprehensive view of how this *Rerum Novarum* current viewed socialism, see 'Is Socialismu — Chelmtejn mis Sur Fons mehudin minn wiehed mill cotba tieghu', *Id-Dawl*, 15 December 1931.
[20] H. Mc Leod, *Religion and the People of Western Europe 1789-1970*, 51.

[U]nione [P]olitica [M]altese and the *[P]artito [D]emocratico [N]azionalista* which contested the Gozo district only. The main social objective of this block was the creation of an organic corporatist movement involving the total hegemony of the Church and the middle classes over the working classes. This ideal began to be propagated in response to the threats which the ruling classes felt coming from a potential reformist alliance between the modernist pro-British middle class and the mass of the workers from the urban areas. In fact on 23 October 1921, the UPM (the party representing the compromising section of the ruling classes, which believed in keeping cordial relations with the colonial authorities as the best guarantee for the surviving of their interests) invited the Labour executive to unite forces for the coming elections. However, the Labour Party turned down this invitation as well as similar invitations from the PDN (in June 1921) and from the Constitutional Party. The Labour executive decided to contest the elections independently.[21] In the 1921 elections, the Labour Party elected seven candidates:

  I District − Vincenzo Farruġia
  II District − Michel Borg
  III District − Michael Dundon and Pier Ġ. Frendo
  IV District − Vincenzo Busuttil, Leone Portelli and Pawlu Borg Grech.[22]

The majority of the elected members belonged to the dominant pro-clerical section. It is not surprising that later, on 9 April 1922, the Labour representatives in the Legislative Assembly backed the UPM in government, during the first Howard administration.[23] This backing developed into a coalition, whereas according to the Leftist perspective this only ensured the hegemony of the ruling privileged classes over the masses. In fact, the dominant pro-clerical Labour leadership, which fully backed the government in power, had nothing to lose in

---

[21] Borg, 34.
[22] Bonnici, 45.
[23] Bonnici, 47.

associating itself with the UPM. It is significant that one conservative politician, Herbert Ganado, interpreted this coalition as the work of practical men in the Labour Party and the UPM 'who believed in compromise in politics so that in giving a little they could move much nearer to each other'.[24] In 1922 Pier Frendo, one of these compromising elements in the Labour Party, wrote a series of articles in his party's organ *Labour Opinion*, which reflected clearly this ideological stand. For instance, the Maltese worker's interests and his ideals were conceived from a corporatist point of view and socialism was seen as its main agressive opponent.[25]

It is not difficult to see that the aim of the clerico-professional Labour leadership which allied with the UPM in government was to keep socialist ideas as far away as possible. However, the alliance was not to last for long because of the grave conflicts within the Labour Party which reflected the emergence of a most important current and a new balance of forces within the same party. A strong progressive reformist trend began germinating underneath the predominantly rightist leadership which conceptualized reforms solely from a Catholic outlook.

This progressive tendency gradually began asserting itself as an organized wing within the Labour quarters and, from the start, attacked the Labour-UPM coalition in government. Their main criticism, viewed from a class-based analysis, was aimed at the economic and social determinants in this coalition. This was seen to be composed of two conflicting class interests which could never fuse harmoniously. In fact, all the promises for reform proved to be nothing more than a set of ideals which were

---

[24] Ganado, 251.
[25] A glaringly clear example of this perspective can be seen from this extract: 'Urge disciplinare bene le organizzazioni operaie, dirigendole verso principii di una vera democrazia cristiana scevia di aspirazioni e propoganda di socialismo. Occorre infondare ai capitalisti e agli operai sensi non di reazione ma di armonia, di avvicinamento. Fa mestieri orientare le corporazioni operaie verso principii sodi, non lasciarle in balia di idee nuove in modo da darsi sempre in braccio su principii di nuovo conio, in modo di abbraciare idee contradittorie e non sane.' P. Frendo, 'L'Idea dell'Operaio Maltese – V.', *Labour Opinion*, 24 August 1922.

doomed to remain on paper. The working classes' more progressive representatives and intellectuals helped to undermine this coalition by demanding immediate and concrete reforms. The fact that a suggested Workman's Compensation Act remained in draft form and never got further than the second reading[26] gave the reformist wing a clearer stand and a greater numerical following among the grass roots.

Ċensu Bugeja, the prominent leftist leader of this developing tendency, wrote from Paris that this was an unnatural coalition that had been made against the interests of the workers and should never have been entered into.[27]

By the time this coalition collapsed, the dominance of the right in the Labour Party had begun diminishing. Mgr. Michael Gonzi had already left the party, while Fr. Ġużè Gatt was not elected after his participation in the first two executives. Canon Carmelo Bugelli, elected member of the national committee of the party in 1922, left the party in 1924 together with James Frendo Azzopardi and Salvu Zammit Hammet, party treasurer since 1923 Fr. Diacono was elected for the third and fourth executives in 1923 while Fr. Egidio Galea Balzan was elected to the Labour executive from 1925 to 1929.

The balance began gradually shifting against the clerical current and in favour of the progressive wing so that, by 1926, the executive began to be numerically dominated by the left.[28]

[26] Borg, 34.
[27] Ċ. Bugeja, 'Il Partit tal Haddiema u il Coalizioni', *Labour Opinion*, 18 January 1923 'It telegramma li waslitilna illum minn Malta għarrafna li il Partit tal Haddiema hall il coalizioni li hua chien ghamel mal "Partito Popolare". Din hia conclusioni wisk logika ta disprezz ta xeukat tal Haddiema fiz-zmien collu li damet din il coalizioni li hia contra in natura u li katt ma chien imissa saret.' [The telegram which reached us today from Malta informed us that the Worker's Party has withdrawn from the coalition which it had entered into with the 'Partito Popolare'. This is the most logical conclusion to the contempt shown for the wishes of the Worker's throughout the time when this coalition held good – a coalition which goes against nature and which should never have taken place.]
[28] See Table 1.

Later on, with the signing of the Compact — Labour's coalition
with the Constitutional — Party, other pro-clerical elements left
the party.[29] As the exit of the clericals and anti-socialists
gathered momentum, another sort of party was developing.[30]

The Compact was felt to be the greatest imaginable threat to
the traditional landowing/professional classes and to the Church.
In 1924 everything showed that the *Partito Democratico Nazionalista* and the *Partito Popolare Maltese (PPM)* were going
to fuse into one single party, gradually developing into a conservative stronghold and collaborating with the local Church
authorities. Soon the Labour Party was to suffer other defections,
as minority anti-compactist groups, remnants of the Catholic
populists, broke away from the party and formed other small
independent entities. Some of these elements formed the *Partit
Nazionali Malti* together with ex-*PPM* members.[31]

The Labour Party which was developing into a progressive party and with the numerical strength of the Constitutional Party
behind it, was to implement Malta's first rudimentary social
legislation. The Compact was naturally described by the political
right as 'socialist', 'protestant' or 'bolshevik'. The local ruling
classes saw in this alliance, among many other dangers, the
threat for the transformation of society to a more secular and
modern one. In it they saw a great challenge to their own vested
interests. A democratic, reformist movement with liberal tendencies was feared and hated just like other similar movements on
the continent.[32]

With the backing of the working classes in the Compact, the
emergent secular pro-British middle class dealt the final blow
to any hopes of the traditional privileged classes to absorb the
Labour Party in its ranks[33] and create a national corporatist

---

[29] *Anon.*, 'It Tradiment Laburista,' *In Nazzion*, 30 January 1926. See also
chapter 3.
[30] See Table 1.
[31] See Appendix A.
[32] G. Spadolini, *L'Opposizione Cattolica*, 28.
[33] Ċ. Bugeja, 'Il Partit tal Haddiema u il Coalizioni'.

movement. However, in the same period (1925 - 1926) when the party was undergoing radical organizational and ideological developments, a more flexible but thoroughly conservative group succeeded again to infiltrate the Labour executive. This group was led by Father Egidio Galea Balzan and Mikiel Caruana and survived in a minority position in the executive until 1930,[34] when they broke away from the party to attempt the creation of an *Independent Labour Party.*

The Left Within the Labour Movement

Some prominent *Dimechians* such as Salvu Astarita who was then the Workers' Union collector of Branch No.3 were very active in the Trade Unions.[35] Many of them worked in the Admiralty dockyard mixing with other 'imported' workers from England and Scotland, some of whom were members of the *Amalgamated Engineering Union.*[36] These contacts stimulated their political ideas.

The Dockyard, the only major industrial complex in Malta, was always the dynamo behind political activities, and a cradle of ideological consciousness. The workers there were always the most ideologically prepared and the most radical.[37]

Dimechianism had strong roots in the Dockyard where socialism and anti-clericalism flourished.[38] The Dockyard was, naturally, the place where the colonial authorities and the Church were always alert for any radical signs. The Labour Party was, in fact, from its beginning successful in the industrial area of the three cities – Senglea, Cospicua, Vittoriosa – where most of the Dockyard workforce came from. In the 1921 elec-

---

[34] See Table 1.
[35] S. Astarita, 'Talba lill Haddiema Maltin', *Il Hmar,* 20 October 1920.
[36] Koster, 87.
[37] As F. Engels states, the assembling of the proleterians in cities where industry could be carried on profitably, 'herding together of great masses in one spot makes the proletarians conscious of their power.' F. Engels, 'Principles of Communism', *Selected Works,* vol.1, 86.
[38] *Il Poplu,* 25 October 1929.

tions, the party won three seats from the Senglea district and another two from the Cospicua – Vittoriosa district.[39]

Leftist propaganda was always surreptiously circulated in the Dockyard, where the workers had direct contacts with British sailors. The *Workers Dreadnought*[40] was for some time also regularly distributed together with other revolutionary literature which was passed 'from hand to hand amongst the workers in such secrecy that it was impossible for Colonial Authorities and their Agents to ascertain from where it came'.[41]

In 1920, Matthew Giles, a representative of the British Workers' Union came to Malta via Gibraltar to visit the existing trade union organisations with instructions from his executive to organize the workers in Branches of the Malta Workers' Union.

On his first visit, at a private meeting of the Imperial Government Workers Union, Giles was reported to have made the following declaration in the course of his address: 'We are out to destroy Government and to instal workers in their place.'[42] His closest friends in Malta were Mikielang Borg, Giacinto Tua, and William Arena, persons described as 'three of the worst agitators in the island'.[43] Later, Giles went to Egypt where he made further contacts with a local revolutionary and the syndicate there, and came to Malta again early in May 1921. Matthew Giles had brought with him large quantities of socialist and communist literature which were also distributed in the

---

[39] J.H. Humphreys, 'Report on the first general elections of general members of the Senate and of members of the Legislative Assembly', *[M]alta [G]overnment [G]azette*, Supplement LIV, 11 November 1921.

[40] The *Workers Dreadnought* was an independent organ which gave support to the Communist Party of Britain from a broader left-wing standpoint. It produced communist and feminist literature and was dominated by Emily Pankhurst. J. Klugmann, *History of the Communist Party of Great Britain*, vol.1, 20,66.

[41] PAV, Churchill to Plumer, 22 June 1921.

[42] *Ibid.*

[43] *Ibid.*

Dockyard.[44] However, during this stay he did not attend any
public meetings 'probably due to the many differences in the
ranks of the Labour Party which have arisen during his absence,
and which no doubt, he is now endeavouring quietly to
remove.'[45]

It was also reported that he failed to unite the Labour factions,
even though he used moderation in his dealings and rhetoric.
He was once insulted in the streets of Valletta by some discharg-
ed Dockyard workers who called him a cheat and an anarchist.
They were so menacing that he had to seek refuge in a shop.[46]

During a first public conference organized by the Labour Party at the De Rohan Band Club at Żebbuġ, Mikielang Borg made
a speech which was interpreted by the pro-clericals as
rebellious.[47] In his speech he addressed the workers in these
words: 'The workers should now break the chains that tie them
in slavery'.[48] The Church immediately reacted by a circular let-

[44] *Ibid.*
[45] PAV, Churchill to Plumer, 28 June 1921.
[46] *Ibid.*
[47] Bonnici, 30.
[48] In another speech delivered in Maltese on 9 December 1920, on the opening
of the first Labour Party headquarters in Valletta, Mikielang Borg says that,
'Il haddiema issa ghandhom ikattu il-ktajjen li bihom jinsabu marbuta fil-jasar...
Jekk ghandhom f'mohhom li s-Socjalismu huwa l'ghajnuna lill haddiema, dak
li jaghmel mezz li n-nies tax-xoghol ikollhom id-dritt ta' xi pensjoni wara li jkunu
ghaddew hajjithom fit-tbatija dak li jipprovdilhom xi indenizzi f'xi dizgrazja,
dak li tnaqsilhom il hinijiet tax-xoghol, dak li ma jithalliex jghabbi t-tfal u n-
niesa b'xoghol li ma jifilhux, jew li dmir il-kapitalist hu li jaghti lil kulhadd
is-salarju li haqqu, ghandhom jiftahru... Sinjuri, jekk dawn il principji huma
principji tas-Socjalismu, jistghu isejhulna kemm iridu socjalisti, ahna zgur li
ma naghmlulhomx citazzjoni per inguria'. Quoted in Ġ. Azzopardi, *Il-Fundaturi
tal-Partit tal-Haddiema.* 3. [The workers should now break the chains that tie
them in slavery... If they believe that Socialism is of help to workers, a means
whereby workmen will earn the right to a pension after a lifetime of hardship,
that which provides them with indemnity after some accident, that which will
obtain shorter working hours, that which will not allow women and children
to be burdened with work which is beyond their ability, that which tells the
capitalist that his duty is to give each and everyone the salary he deserves, then
they should feel proud... Gentlemen, if these principles are socialist principles,
then they are free to call us socialists as much as they want, we shall most
certainly not take them to court for libel.]

ter which outrightly condemned this speech.[49] It was known that leftist elements, some of them *Dimechians*, others staunch socialists and militant anti-clericals, were active in the Labour Party.[50] Mikielanġ Borg had been assistant secretary of the *Comitato Patriottico*[51], and an ardent patriot and playwright in Maltese.

On 27 December 1923, *Labour Opinion* announced on its front page the death of Michaelangelo Refalo.[52] Refalo's speech in favour of the weak and of the working classes, on the occasion of the Succession Taxes Debates, reflect his deep humanism.[53] Refalo maintained that the workers should not be used as instruments for the enrichment of the minority. Social insurance and social services had to be immediately introduced. The proletariat should be educated to fight for its own rights, not only to accept the security of a bed in the state hospital after being injured by the machinery of some big industrialist. Through education, the proletariat would understand that its rights included much more than the opportunity to eat and rest in an old people's institute after a lifetime's work to fatten the pocket of some speculator.[54] Refalo was to be quoted innumerable times by Compact propagandists, who made use of his speeches to push forward the movement's objectives.

---

[49] Ganado, 243.
[50] *Ibid.*
[51] Frendo, 185.
[52] M.A. Refalo (1876 - 1923) had been decorated with the title 'Commander of the British Empire' for his outstanding merits in the First World War. In 1919 he was nominated Chief Justice of the Law Courts and President of the Court of Appeal. He had also been the main instigator and legislator for succession taxes in Malta. R. Mifsud Bonnici, *Dizzjunarju Bijo-Bibliografiku Nazzjonali*, 430.
[53] *Anon.*, 'Refalo u il Fkir', *Labour Opinion*, 3 January 1924: '...allura scont chif jahsbu dauc li huma contra din it-taxxa, chiecu il Gvern ġieb kuddiem progett ta liġi biex jipprovdi l-istess ghal bżonnijiet tal-caxxa u irrisparmia b'mezzi mghaugia il classijiet ghonia allura ghandi nahseb li il politica tal gvern ma chienitx tkun la goffa u ankas jebsa, iżda chienet tcun politica helua u bl'inguanti!' [...thus, according to the way of thinking of those who are against this tax, had Government promoted draft legislation to provide similarly for the requirements of the Treasury and used crooked means to exempt the monied classes, I am to think that the Government's policy would have been neither heavy handed nor hard, it would have been a sweet velvet-gloved policy!]
[54] *Ibid.*

After the return of Matthew Giles (1921) and the organization of the Labour Party, the leftists, who were, by this time, termed 'extremists',[55] were rather few in number, and some of them no longer contested as committee members after serving in the first consecutive executives.[56] They viewed with consternation the growing influence of the Church among the workers who were members of the Workers' Union. According to the agents of the colonial authorities, the leftists tried hard to counteract the Church's influence, by continuous propaganda, as instructed by Giles.[57]

This section of the leftist militants were centred around Censu Bugeja, the leading radical intellectual who lived in Paris, but who often came to Malta. He wrote regularly in Maltese with a very radical pen on the local political situation. This section in the Labour Party was seen as the most intelligent, with the leadership in touch with the methods and tactics of the workers' movements abroad.[58] Bugeja was also the assistant editor of the European edition of *The New York Herald Tribune*,[59] and wrote in many other foreign journals. He came to the forefront of Maltese politics with an article-manifesto entitled 'For a Labour Programme' which he wrote for the *Daily Malta Chronicle* of 22 June 1921. In this article, Bugeja makes clear his conception of a workers' party, as he believed that its aims were beginning to be misunderstood. According to Bugeja, Labour should reject philanthropy and should strive for the workers' rights. The political forces around Labour had of necessity to be organized as an autonomous force with definite objectives and with its own designated tactics. It had to work for the advancement of the economic interests of the workers within democratic channels. However, owing to the capitalist system,

---

[55] Borg, 28.
[56] PAV, Churchill to Plumer, 28 June 1921.
[57] PAV, Churchill to Plumer, 22 June 1921.
[58] Seven Wise Men, 'Divisions in the Labour Party', *Malta Herald* 24 October 1923.
[59] Azzopardi, *Il-Fundaturi tal-Partit tal-Haddiema*, 107.

it was soon discovered that without a radical transformation on which
the state has been built, there was no hope of raising the working classes
from the low economic conditions to which they were condemned by
an inherently bad social system.[60]

This article-programme raised a strong reaction from the
church. Mgr. Canon Enrico Dandria, a leading priest politician, in answer to Bugeja's thesis, assured the people that
Bugeja was a

socialist with tendencies towards collectivism and sympathies for
Anarchy and Bolshevism, at least as for achieving a radical revolution
which he has not even the prudence to call evolution.[61]

Being the leading intellectual of the leftist wing in the party,
Bugeja was one of the main opponents of coalition with the local
upper classes. He had been the most intransigent opponent of
the Labour coalition with the UPM in government. In his view
such a coalition could only propagate the privileges and the
power of the ruling classes, and would even endanger the
autonomy of the Labour Party as the party striving solely for
the interests of the working classes.[62] Censu Bugeja took this
argument to its logical conclusion and demanded concrete
conditions and assurances of an 'unquestionably proletarian
character', (such as sanitary improvements, raising of the
standard of living, educational reforms and non-capitalist
solutions to the problems of unemployment) in order to sign any
coalition.[63]

---

[60] Bugeja continues 'No blood-shedding or destruction of property is
contemplated especially in Malta where the resistence of an obstinate capitalist
minority is unthinkable. But it would be to distort the idea of the Labour
Movement if it were described otherwise than as revolutionary. Its aim is to
bring about a social order so different from that in which we have been born
and lived our lives so far, that future historians will not apply any other term
to it than Revolution. By peaceful democratic means it may take years to
establish it, but the final result will be none the less a revolution.' C. Bugeja,
' For a Labour Programme', *Daily Malta Chronicle*, 22 June 1921.
[61] E. Dandria, 'The Maltese Socialist', *Daily Malta Chronicle*, 27 June 1921.
[62] C. Bugeja, 'Il Partit tal Haddiema u l Coalizioni': 'Ma haun l-ebda dubju li
'L'Unione' hasbet li hia tista tassorbixxi il partit tal Haddiema, iżda dan il partit
wera biċċar li hua behsiebu jimxi ghalieh u ghal dakshekk hua ta min jifrahlu.'
[There is no doubt that 'L'Unione' thought that it could absorb the Workers'
Party, but the latter has shown clearly that it intends to forge ahead on its own,
and for this reason it ought to be congratulated.]
[63] C. Bugeja, 'For a Labour Programme'.

By this time many of the founding members were no longer active among the Labour leadership.[64] In fact, from among the founding members of the party, only William Savona and Ġanni Bencini were confirmed as party officials in the second executive.[65] As a result, the character of the leadership changed dramatically; a change which reflected the dynamic development of the party's grass roots.

From 1921 to 1925 William Savona served as president on the Party's executive. Another ardent activist was Mosè Gatt who served as member of the executive from 1922 to 1925.[66]

In 1925 the balance, however, began to tilt in favour of the more radical elements, when a number of left wingers found their way into the sixth executive. Ġużè Orlando, who had been a member of the general committee, was chosen as secretary of the party. Ġino Muscat Azzopardi,[67] was also elected for the first time to the executive and given the post of assistant secretary. In the eighth executive, Muscat Azzopardi was nominated editor of the party's official newspaper.

Between 1924 and 1926 the most prominent clerical elements resigned from the Labour executive. Ġużè Ellul and John F. Marks, both of them socialists, were elected to the executive committee for the first time in 1926. In this year also, Etelualdo Bugeja, an anti-clerical activist, was nominated treasurer.[68] By 1928, the most important positions in the Labour Party were all held by the left. The executive remained dominated by the left until the early 1930s when Salvu Pulis and Wiġi Azzopardi (both members of the Socialist League) were elected to the executive.[69]

---

[64]*Anon., Il-Qawmien tal-Haddiem Malti*, vol.1, 5,13.
[65] Bonnici, 52.
[66] See Table 1.
[67] Ġino Muscat Azzopardi was later labelled by the colonial authorities a leftist, associating with local communists. PAV Des. No.60, Gov. D. Campbell to SSC P. Cuncliffe Lister, 3 April 1933: 'Gino Muscat Azzopardi, was known to be in touch with the members of the local communist organisation. When the Soviet trade commissar, visited Malta in 1931, Gino Muscat Azzopardi was in close touch with him. Gino Muscat Azzopardi was a paying member of the clandestine circulating library consisting of subversive literature... He associates with members of the local communist organization.'
[68] See Table 1.
[69] *Ibid.*

The year 1925 was a significant one for the Labour Party. In this year the party had two executives because a number of its members and party founders who had been elected to the first 1925 executive resigned. These were Ġanni Bencini, Vincenzo Farrugia, George Hersey, Alfredo Portelli, William Savona, Ġanni Scerri, Anton Schembri, and Oliver St.John.[70] These resignations followed the exit of the pro-clerical old guard of the party who had unsuccessfully contested the first 1925 Labour Party executive election a few months before. The unsuccessful canditates were Dr. Ġużè Ellul, Alfons Maria Borg, James Frendo Azzopardi and Salvu Zammit Hammett. This meant that a complete change took place in the Labour executive in 1925 − in fact, only Paul Borg Grech LL.D., Ġużè Calleja, Mosè Gatt, Ġino Muscat Azzopardi, Ġużè Orlando, and Mikielanġ Borg kept their seats in the second 1925 executive, the last three being well-known leftist elements. The party emerged from these events into the second half of the twenties and the early thirties with a constant leftist majority among its leadership, namely Mikielanġ Borg, Ġużè Ellul Mercer, John F. Marks, Ġino Muscat Azzopardi, and Ġużè Orlando.[71] This transformation brought with it ideological and structural changes in the party. In a meeting held on 31 August 1925,[72] the representatives of band clubs were eliminated while the other societies, dominated by professionals and clerics, were given secondary importance to the district committees. Ġużè Orlando (who was elected secretary general when he was first elected to the executive in 1925) led the reorganization commission which gave more power to the grass root committees of the party[73] and attempted to break the strength of the pro-clerical religio-populist current in the Labour Party. Ċensu Bugeja wrote from Paris to say that it was only then that the Labour Party had cleaned itself of opportunists

[70] *Ibid.*
[71] Bonnici, 95, 98.
[72] Present in the first meeting of the new executive were, amongst others, Ġużè Orlando as secretary, Mikielanġ Borg returning as member, Ġino Muscat Azzopardi as his assistant secretary, William Savona as president and Mosè Gatt also as one of the members. See Table 1.
[73] Bonnici, 97.

and that it was really becoming a party which truly represented the workers.[74]

This transformation in the leadership was not only reflected in the reorganization of the party's structure. Change in the ideological outlook could be seen in the party's political manifesto. The 1925 programme declared the party to be in favour of the abolition of the senate. The party also declared itself against taxation on necessary materials for the country's industries, and against tax on wheat. On the other hand the party was in favour of (and sought to promote) a one-man-one-vote franchise, compulsory education and the teaching of technical skills. Some basic social laws which this programme wanted enacted were essentially the same as those in the preceding programmes namely the Workmen's Compensation Act and the Trade Union Act, while it also desired certain corrections and amendments in the Rent and the Electoral Laws. This 1925 electoral programme, which was drafted by a selected commission, contained moreover a declaration that the Labour Party would work with the Constitutional Party to gain power and pass social legislation.[75] In fact, this particular 1925 executive had the responsibility of negotiating a Compact with the Constitutionalists.

---

[74] Ċ. Bugeja, 'The Existing Order of Things', *Labour Opinion,* 15 October 1925. 'Ippermettili nesprimi l ferh tieghi bl'organizzazjoni l-gdida tal Partit tghana, bl'idejiet li l-partit gharaf jibbraccia u bil leaders kapaċi li għażel. Mil-lum il-quddiem il-partit hua il-veru partit tal-haddiema mehlus min dawk li ma kellhomx l'intelligenza sabiex jgharfu x'inhuma l-bżonnijiet veri tal-haddiema Maltin, u mill banda l'ohra minn dawk li hasbu jistghu jisservew bil-haddiema sabiex jghamlu xi sold mill politka.' [Permit me to express my pleasure with our Party's new organisation, with the ideas which the party has exposed and the able leaders he has chosen. From today onwards the party is the real Worker's party, freed of those who were not sufficiently intelligent to realise the real needs of the Maltese workers, and, on the other hand, also freed of those who thought they could use the workers and line their pockets by going in for politics.]
[75] Bonnici, 98-99.

Intellectual Avant-garde

A favourite meeting place of leftist intellectuals was the *Cafè Regina*, or Cafè Premier, in Valletta. Here, every evening Gużè Ellul, Ġino Muscat Azzopardi, Ġużè Orlando and Mikielanġ Borg used to meet and discuss politics.[76] All of them were literati: novelists, poets and playwrights. In fact the Labour movement had in its ranks an artistic intellectual avant-garde. Apart from these four personalities, there were others such as Nazzareno Carabott, Nikol Biancardi, two of the many essayists and poets writing in the vernacular; Tancred Ellul, a socio-realist short-story writer; and Ġużè Gatt, a popular historian who, in the twenties and thirties, published innumerable works and articles in many journals and newspapers as well as numerous pamphlets. The most significant common feature was that they all wrote in their native Maltese language.

Some of their works met with the disapproval of the ecclesiastical authorities. For example the Archbishop censured as immoral Ġużè Ellul's novel, *Bniedem,* from his series 'Il Hrejjef ta' Barraminau', published in *Il Hmar* in 1928. Ċensu Bugeja's article *'Haddiema! Ngħakkdu il ponnijiet'* was also censured.[77] Mikielanġ Borg's *Indipendenza* theatre company was long-lived and his plays in the vernacular were full of sarcasm and skits on the authorities and the dominant classes.[78] Some of his plays also met with strong ecclesiastical disapproval.

Other leftist literature included Ġino Muscat Azzopardi's socio-realistic works, as were the novels of Ġużè Orlando, Ġużè Ellul, and John F. Marks. This socio-realistic literary movement was consonant with the ideological transformation of the Labour Party. The literary and theatrical works of these intellectuals,

---

[76] M. Azzopardi, 'Socio-Realisti Madwar Ellul Mercer', *Mis-Sillabu,* vol.1 144.
[77] Circular 227, 11 December 1928, in D. Mintoff *'Journalism in Malta, An account and appreciation'* 567.
[78] Mikielanġ Borg, *Karambola, gabra ta' ittri u artikli f'gurnali li wara li jolqtu lilna jduru kollha fuq il-Kumpanija Filodrammatika l'Indipendenza',* 17.

together with Juann Mamo's publications, such as *Ulied in Nanna Venut fl'Amerca*, manifested avant-garde political tendencies and objectives. Their primary aims were those of communicating with the masses, educating them and instilling in them political awarness. The new workers' movement was the place for all intellectuals, scientists, poets and artists.

You poets, painters, sculptors, musicians, if you have understood your mission in the world and the real interests of your own art, come and join us. Put your pen, brush, chisel and your ideas to serve the poor. Use your artistic ability to show the struggle of the people against its oppressor.[79]

This intellectual elite saw the traditional literary styles as decadent and escapist from the real problems of life. Juann Mamo wrote that ignorance should be fought by literary means by 'good men and priests', but these did not want to communicate with the people and all they thought and wrote about was on themes which did not really interest the people.[80] Literature was to be used to educate the masses as a means to emancipate them from ignorance and superstition. The most common literary themes dealt with in the works of these authors showed their ideological orientation. The most popular subjects were militarism and war, as the consequence of a degenerate

---

[79] Guże Orlando, *Liż-żagħżagħ*, 15: 'Intom poeti, pitturi, sculturi, muzicisti, jekk fhimtu l-missjoni tagħcom fid-dinja, u l-istess interessi ta' l-arti tagħcom stess, ejjew magħna. Kiegħdu l-pinna, pinżell, scarpell u l-ideat tagħcom għas-servizz tal-fqar. Uruna bil-ħila artistika tagħcom it-taqbida tal-poplu contra l-oppressuri tiegħu.'

[80] J. Mamo, *Ulied in Nanna Venut fl'Amerca*, 'bħas Sur Fons Galea, Dun Saidon, Dun C. Psaila, ecc., imma daun hsiebhom biex jimxu wara 'l-bidwi li jizra f'art m'hix maħduma, hsiebhom fil chitba li l-poplu mħolli b'mod li ma jifimhiex, jeu jakraha iva, u jifimha daks pappagal! Imberichalla ! Trid tgħid – J.M.' [like Mr. Alphons Galea, Father Saidon, Father C. Psaila, etc., but these are bent on following after the farmer who sows his seed in untilled land, they are intent on writing in a manner that the people, deprived of proper schooling, are unable to understand, or can read it, but understand it no better than a parrot would! Praise be to God! That is what you ought to say – J.M.]

capitalism,[81] ignorance, the incapacity to live a fully human life in misery; and the need for education and enlightenment of the people to emancipate themselves.[82] But literature alone would do nothing to elevate the masses from misery, for it cannot change reality by itself. They knew that the practical means to change society had to be political. Writing in Maltese had also to be accompanied by the building of schools, compulsory education and the campaign to have Maltese accepted as the official language of the country.[83]

For many on the left, the language question (whether to adopt English or Italian as the official language of the Maltese Islands) had been a contrived and artificial one, as the workers, in their great majority, spoke only Maltese. According to one of these Labour intellectuals, the Italian language was the mainstay of class domination in Malta.'[84]

Towards Socialism and Progress

The transformation of the Labour Party was therefore not only structural but also ideological.[85] The men who came to the forefront of the Labour leadership in 1925/26 were ideologically oriented to the left. Socialist propaganda increased as a result of Matthew Giles' stay in Malta.

Reports of such 'red propaganda' were frequent in the local papers.[86] However foreign propaganda was not the only type of propaganda which was being circulated in the island. Some *Dimechians* were still preaching their beliefs in the Dockyard, in the Labour Party, and even in the Constitutional Party. Many of them had been writing in Dimechian newspapers while others wrote in other newspapers and periodicals. All were very prolific. Many of them had undergone an ideological transformation

---

[81] Ġ. Ellul Mercer, *Leli ta' Ħaż-Żgħir,* 116.
[82] Mamo, 1930.
[83] *Electoral Programme of the Labour Party,* Malta, 1925.
[84] J.F. Marks, 'Class Domination and the Language Question', *Il Hmar,* 27 May 1931.
[85] Ċ. Bugeja, 'The Existing Order of Things'.
[86] L-Editur, 'Labour jew Socialisti ?', *Il-Progress,* 1 February 1924.

orienting themselves more to socialism. The Dimechian Salvu Zammit frequently wrote in Maltese newspapers on this subject. He asserted that a party which called itself a 'workers' party' but did not have a socialist programme was not genuine.[87]

In this same newspaper of Dimechian inspirations, *Malta tal Maltin*, other pro-socialist articles were published. One such article *Is Socialismu* summarizes the concept of socialism in the following words:

socialism is an economic doctrine, it is that scientific organization that satisfies man's necessities.[88]

The people needed houses, clothes, food and their own fields to cultivate. The country needed industries which had to be directed to the needs of the people. Land had to be nationalized. If the government was not prosperous enough to begin the industrialization of the country, it had to force the capitalists to utilize their capital, even though the social programme was always opposed to individualistic capitalism because such profits went into the pockets of the minority who did not work.[89]

Industrialization was one of the most important aspirations which a social reformist party had to select as its main objective. With industrialization, society would inevitably change. Many believed that the existing order of things would be destroyed and the standard of living of the working masses would be raised to a civilized level.[90] On this point many intellectuals of the Maltese working-class were in agreement with the liberal progressive pro-British middle class, politically represented in the Constitutional Party. Declarations from middle-class quarters ensued:

[87] S. Zammit, 'Chemm hua mehtieg is Socialismu', *Malta tal Maltin,* 19 April 1924.
[88] Bona Fide Worker, 'Is-Socialismu', *Malta tal Maltin,* 3 May 1924: 'Is-Socialismu hua dottrina economica, hua dic l'organizzazjoni xientifica li tissodisfa il bżonn tal bniedem, numru cbir ta nies jinsabu ansiusi biex icunu jafu x'inhua dan is-socialismu'. [Socialism is an economic doctrine, it is that scientific organisation which satisfies man's needs. A large number of people are eager to find out what this socialism actually is.]
[89] *Ibid.*
[90] F. Azzopardi, 'Socialisti!', *Labour Opinion,* 11 November 1925.

Let the true leader of the Labour Party, who aims at the full attainment of the contentment and happiness of his followers, bravely unmask the enemy. Let the Labour component of imported manufactured goods be minutely analysed, and let a judicious, efficient protective duty be imposed and so build a barrier against the common enemy'.[91]

They insisted that the interests of the industrialists and the workers matched. For them, the common enemy were the importers and a protective duty against importation was necessary for the development of Maltese industry. According to this view, industrialization would bring a progressive transformation in the lives of the people, as it would uplift and educate the Maltese in a flourishing economic state.[92]

The Labour and Constitutional policies in this respect had very much in common. In fact this was the real basis upon which the 1926 Compact between the Constitutionals and the Labour Party was to be signed.

In the Labour programme written by Ċensu Bugeja in 1921, great emphasis had been placed on an ultimate objective of the workers' movement:

Once Labour is in power the privileged few who now benefit by the work of the many will sooner or later disappear and the state will exist merely for workers. The ideal of Labour is to replace the class state by the Labour state.[93]

The Constitutional Party, according to Bugeja's analysis, was a party full of businessmen and of all those who were pro-British, ex-officers and servicemen, and those who had been educated in England. On the other hand, he saw the Constitutional party as counterbalancing the other parties of the traditional privileged classes[94] — who were seeking to Italianize Malta. However according to him, Labour had to pay great attention in signing any alliance with the Constitutionals.[95]

[91] Protectionist, 'Protection of Free Trade', *Daily Malta Chronicle*. 25 June 1921.
[92] *Ibid.*
[93] Ċ. Bugeja, 'For a Labour Programme'.
[94] V. Bugeja, 'Letter from Paris', *Labour Opinion*, 21 December 1923.
[95] Ċ. Bugeja, 'For a Labour Programme'.

Ċensu Bugeja's concept of nationalism was very different from that held by Fortunato Mizzi. Bugeja condemned the Mizzi type of nationalism because it tended to keep a class-divided society with a huge economic and social gap between the dominant classes and the masses.[96] On the other hand, Ċensu Bugeja believed that nationalism was a process that should start with the masses not with the upper classes. This was a 'natural' process which the more progressive European countries had gone through.[97] In a historical political analysis, written in 1931, John F. Marks stated that the Constitutional Party was to be admired for its stand against the interference of the Church in secular matters.[98] Marks stated that the Constitutionals had inherited this 'progressive enlightened vision' from the true nationalists of 1892 led by Mizzi.

The Anglo-Maltese Independent Labour Party.

In 1924, a newspaper, the *Malta Labour Leader* was launched by the Anglo-Maltese Independent Labour Party (AMILP) which in that same year had affiliated with the British Independent Labour Party (ILP).[99]

The ILP had been founded in Britain in 1893 as a socialist body. Since then it had been the main driving force in the formation of the Labour Representative Committee and later the British Labour Party.[100] It initially had the support of F. Engels and E. Aveling who helped to draw up its programme.[101] The British ILP had evolved from a position that attempted to reconcile socialism and unionism to a party

---

[96] Ċ. Bugeja, 'Malta Nazion', *Labour Opinion'* 18 June 1925.
[97] *Ibid.* 'Il veru nazzionalizmu ma jistax icun monopolju fl'idejn classi, izda ghandu johrog minn poplu shieh li induna li ghandu xeukat u interessi komuni'. [True nationalism cannot be a monopoly left in the hands of one class, but must emanate from a whole people that has discovered it has commom aspirations and interests.]
[98] J.F. Marks, 'Class Domination and the Language Question'.
[99] Uihed li jaf il cullhatt, 'It Trionf ta' l'Independent Labour Party', *Malta Labour Leader,* 27 September 1924.
[100] Klugmann, vol.1, 25.
[101] H. Pelling, *The Origins of the Labour Party 1880-1900,* 219.

of left-wing socialists who disliked the conservatism of the British Labour leaders and wanted a socialist alternative.[102] In the 1920s the British ILP had become an ardent socialist group which disassociated itself from the British Labour Party by a conference decision.[103]

This was the situation in Britain when a number of Maltese socialists, impatient with the pro-clerical leadership in the Maltese Labour Party united to form the AMILP on the left of the Labour Party.[104] Some of the prominent personalities who founded the AMILP were: Salvu Zammit, Ġużè Scicluna, Carl Zammid, Joseph Pace and Joe Grech.[105]

From the content of their writing and from the lists of imported books and pamphlets, it is clear that they were influenced by British socialists such as Keir Hardie, Philip Snowden, H.G. Wells, and G.D.H. Cole.[106] Yet, like its mother party in Britain, it declared itself to be as constitutional as it was revolutionary in character:

Within the limits of Constitutionalism, however, it seemed to be determined to fight its battles without compromise. It paid for its own politics, and was not afraid to publish its balance-sheet to the world. It was this which made the political scientist Ostrogorski describe it as "a novel phenomenon in the life of English party organization".[107]

The AMILP's ideological stand was that of its mother party in Britain: a type of sentimental socialism; hatred of the capitalist system; and a faith in a kind of spontaneous socialism.[108] The AMILP's socialism was declared to have nothing in common with communism and did not propagate any bureaucratic system of government. It declared its adherence to a genre of humanitarian socialism:

---

[102] H. Pelling, *A Short History of the Labour Party*, 55.
[103] *Ibid.*
[104] C. Zammit, interviewed by the author, 21 March 1986.
[105] Some of these had also been founding members of the short-lived *Ghakda Progressiva tal Haddiema, Malta tal Maltin*, 28 September 1922.
[106] S. Zammit, 'New Publications', *Malta Labour Leader*, 28 September 1924.
[107] Pelling, *The origins of the Labour Party* 219.
[108] Klugmann, vol.1, 26.

Maltese Socialism is not blind to human weaknesses and not deaf to the needs of the workers that form the rights of living, because these are the fundamental bases of the AMILP and for it, it will be responsible.[109]

The Maltese socialists believed in the International Socialist Movement and hoped that the local workers would unite and act, as their brothers in more enlightened countries had already done.[110]

As soon as the AMILP was formed, the Church attacked it as a Protestant society.[111] Its members were labelled bolsheviks and revolutionaries,[112] and the Church could have excommunicated them were it not for the party's direct affiliation with the British ILP. In fact, from the AMILP's emergence it was already rumoured that the members were going to be excommunicated by the Catholic Church.[113] Some fervent opponents of the AMILP came from the conservative front of the Labour Party, led by Canon Carmelo Bugelli.[114]

The AMILP's members believed that the only way to raise the standard of living of the people was to gear the economy to the process of industrialization. To do this, the wealthy Maltese should become entrepreneurs and capitalists, on the American and English models, and invest their capital in manufacturing

[109] J. Pace, 'X'inhu s Socializmu', *Malta Labour Leader,* 6 September 1924, 'Is Socialismu hua il propieta ta metodu fil haija mil poplu ghal poplu minflok mil profiteers ghal profiteers. Hua il control ta l'industria mill haddiema minn floc mill'esploitaturi; minn dauc li jafu hafna riguard l'industria minn floc minn dauc li jafu ftit fuka.' [Socialism is a way of life managed by the people for the people, instead of it being run by profiteers for profiteers. It is the control of industry by workers instead of exploiters, by those who know a great deal about industry rather than those who know little about it.]
[110] J. Smith, 'Socialism'. *Malta Labour Leader,* 13 September 1924.
[111] *Anon.,* 'The Language of the Worker's Evolution', *Malta Labour Leader,* 13 September 1924.
[112] *Anon.,* 'Ir-Religion, il Costituzioni u il Professionisti', *Malta Labour Leader,* 13 September 1924.
[113] *Ibid.*
[114] *Anon.,* 'Trijonf tal I.L.P.', *Malta Labour Leader,* 27 November 1924, 'malli chien jaf li l'Anglo Maltese Independent Labour Party affiliat ma l'I.L.P. ta' l'Ingilterra malajr ghamel interpellanza lill gvern ta Malta biex ma thalliex il dan il partit jicber.' [as soon as he got to know that the Anglo Maltese Labour Party is affiliated to the British I.L.P. he immediately called upon the government of Malta to see to it that this policy does not grow in strength.]

industries and therefore expand employment opportunities.[115] The privileged classes should reinvest their capital from foreign banks in local manufacturing industry. If the traditional Maltese bourgeoisie was not ready to invest its capital in Malta, a future workers' government, would legislate in favour of imposing an enormous levy on all capital invested in foreign countries by wealthy Maltese.[116] Industrialization should be planned on socialist principles because the intention of socialism is to get rid of poverty and immorality.[117] Workers had to have control of industries and the consumers had to have a valid say in whatever they bought. The AMILP's socialism was not that type which postulated to control industries with the state's bureaucracy.[118] They had no intention of creating state-controlled industries, as those whom they termed 'extremists' wanted. In fact in one of the most interesting articles written in the Maltese language in the *Malta Labour Leader* (the AMILP's organ), it was stated that the AMILP was not a revolutionary organization but was going to fight capitalism by legal means.[119]

The AMILP wanted only to manifest the nobility of work and to strive for workers' rights.[120] In fact British Independent Labour Party (ILP) leaders like Keir Hardie ignored Marxism and rejected class struggle in theory, even if they carried it out in practice.[121] However, the AMILP's programme in these years had a more progressive outlook than that of the Maltese Labour Party. [122]   It wanted:

---

[115] J. Grech, 'Lill Capitalisti Maltin', *Malta Labour Leader,* 8 November 1924.
[116] *Ibid.*
[117] Socialista Kalbieni, 'Harsa fuk is Socialismu', *Malta Labour Leader,* 4 October 1924.
[118] S. Zammit, 'Is Socializmu − x'inhu, x'mahux u x'irid,' *Malta Labour Leader*, 6 September 1924.
[119] J. Grech, 'Lil Capitalisti Maltin'.
[120] Anon., 'Haddiema Maltin', *Malta Labour Leader*, 6 September 1924.
[121] Klugmann, vol. 1., 26.
[122] S. Zammit, 'Is Socializmu − x'inhu, x'mahux u x'irid'.

1. Employment for all
2. Old age pensions
3. Women's pensions
4. Maltese as an official language
5. Supremacy of the English and Maltese languages
6. A fixed wage for all
7. Technical schools and public libraries
8. Government financial assistance to emigrants
9. Houses for the workers
10. Abolition of plural voting
11. Industrialization
12. Opening of the university for working class children.[123]

As regards land, the AMILP wanted this to become the common property of the community, while enterprises should ideally also belong to the people.[123] These aspirations, the Maltese socialists believed, were to become a reality because the Maltese workers had the support of millions of Anglo-Saxon workers who were affiliated to the British ILP.[124]

However as an affiliated branch to the British ILP, the AMILP members believed that they had good protection from the British authorities.[125] The party's activists contended that their opponents, coming from the ruling classes and from the pro-clerical Labour leadership, were traitors of the working classes.[126] They considered them despots whose main interest was to leave the masses in ignorance and reap profits from their work.[127]

The party had been organized in 1924, the year in which the Labour Party was in coalition with the *Partito Popolare Maltese*. In fact this was one of the causes that led to the formation of the AMILP, which was made up of elements that rejected any

[123] Socialista Kalbieni, 'Harsa fuk is Socialismu'
[124] Anon., 'Il Kuddiem', *Malta Labour Party*, 6 September 1924.
[125] S. Zammit, 'Is Socializmu – x'inhu, x'mahux u x'irid'.
[126] Uihed li jaf lil culhatt, 'It Trijonf ta' l'Independent Labour Party'.
[127] J. Smith, 'Socialism'.

compromise with the traditional clerico-professional classes. It reminded its opponents that they then enjoyed an advantageous position with the British government as, in January 1924, the King had called upon Ramsay MacDonald to form a cabinet, which he did with the support of the Labour Party. (MacDonald had been a leading personality in the british ILP.) Furthermore, the AMILP, time and again reminded their political enemies that they did not want the 1921 constitution which, in their view, hindered the emancipation of the working classes.[128]

The existence of an organization such as the AMILP is very interesting. However, one should not overlook the fact that the AMILP members were few and that the organization was short-lived. In fact these founding members, led by Salvu Zammit, were just a small nucleus who were trying to organize themselves in a mass-party.[129] However, they were much more influential than their number suggests not only because of the circulation of the Maltese organ, the *Malta Labour Leader*, but also because of the books and pamphlets imported from Britain and which evidently were widely read. (References to them in local newspapers, periodicals, and books were abundant.)[130] These greatly influenced the intellectual climate of the pre-Compact years.[131]

---

[128] *Anon.*, 'Ir Religion, il Costituzioni u il Professionisti': 'Nitolbu ucoll lill dauc collha li ghandhom li schiedi li hrigna, jghaglu jimleuhom bl'ismijet ta hbiebhom, u tahhom, biex meta jasal iz-zmien, ga la darba keghdin jistmauna ta kabda bhejjem intaijru l'icbar cuccanja li katt setghu joholmu biha il professionisti, il costituzioni!' [We also ask all those who have copies of the forms we issued, to hasten to fill in their names and those of their friends, so that, when the time comes, seeing that we are being treated like a herd of beasts, we will do away with the greatest obscenity the members of the professions could ever think of − the constitution!]

[129] *Anon.*, 'Il Kuddiem'

[130] *Vide L'Idea Socialista.*

[131] Books in circulation were written by such authors as Hardie, Snowden, Gordon, Cole, etc. One of the lists published by the *Malta Labour Leader* cites the following pamphlets which were for sale at two pence each: Brockway, A. Fenner. *How to End War;* Dalton, Hugh. *Will Capital Leave the Country?;* Henderson, Fred. *The Socialism of the I.L.P.;* Johnson, Francis. *Keir Hardie's Socialism;* Mos, J. M.P. *Municipal Banks and How to Run Them;* Mc Arthur, Archie. *Socialism and Religion: A Plea for Both;* Macdonald, J. Ramsay, M.P. *Why*

The majority of these AMILP socialists later joined the Compact. Their literature was widely read in Labour circles, in the Dockyard, and later within other leftist groups. In the maltese Labour Party, the british ILP principles were later to be expounded by such prominent personalities as Ġużè Orlando, George Ernest Geoghegan and Carmelo Zammit.

The british ILP's Protestant inspiration also made a mark on the maltese political arena.[132] The Protestant ethic was inherited by the AMILP. Poverty for them did not simply mean the lack of necessities of life, but more importantly, the immoral life which workers were forced to lead as a result of the poor conditions they lived in.[133] The emphasis on the necessity of industrialization was combined with the need for local entrepreneurs to invest productively in the economy of their own country, instead of accumulating their money in foreign banks. This would create an expansive proletarian class and produce a progressive industrial bourgeoisie which, like its prototypes in Britain and the northern countries, would be capable of becoming an autonomous national bourgeoisie. Only then would this new bourgeoisie replace the traditional parasitic ruling classes which were incapable of creating the conditions for industrialization.

These ideological trends were attacked by the church in Malta, which labelled the AMILP as a Protestant society.[134] Notwithstanding these attacks, however, such trends were later to flow with ease within the reformist movement's main stream of ideas.

Socialism Must Come; Morel, E.D., M.P. *The Poison that Destroys;* Snowden, Philip, M.P. *The Individual Under Socialism;* Snowden, Philip, M.P. *Socialism Made Plain;* Snowden, Philip, M.P. *The Economic Case for Socialism;* Sparkes, Malcolm. *How Socialism Would Run Industry;* Walker, R.B. *Speed the Plough;* S. Zammit, 'Pamphlets', *Malta Labour Leader,* 8 November 1924.

[132] Pelling, *The Origins of the Labour Party,* 135.

[133] Socialista Kalbieni, 'Harsa fuk is Socialismu'.

[134] *Anon.,* 'The Language of the Workers' Evolution', *Malta Labour Leader,* 13 September 1924.

THE
MALTA LABOUR LEADER

OFFICIAL ORGAN OF THE ANGLO-MALTESE INDEPENDENT LABOUR PARTY
MALTA BRANCH OF THE BRITISH I. L. P.

All the past we leave behind,
We debouch upon a newer, mightier world, varied world,
Fresh and strong the world we seize, world of labour and
the march,
Pioneers! O pioneers!

WALT WHITMAN

Editor: SALVO ZAMMIT.
70, Str. San Giovanni—Cospicua.

1st YEAR.   SATURDAY 6th SEPTEMBER 1924.   NUMBER 1.

Ghal min irid jissieheb fl "Malta Labour Leader."

IL KUDDIEM

ID-DEBBA
TAJ-SOCIALISMU F'MALTA

A. M. I. L. P.
X' inhu Is-Socialismu

J. PACE

The first page of Issue no. 1 of The Malta Labour Leader, 6thSeptember, 1924.

3

The Compact

The Labour Party was requested to form coalitions by all political parties which had contested the 1921 elections. The proposals to these invitations — which in a way confirmed the political strength gained by the Labour Party from the very outset[1] — were not accepted by the party. However, the dominant pro-clerical current in the Labour Party led by its parliamentary group later actually reached a coalition with the PPM in government.[2] Because the Labour parliamentary group backed the Howard (26 October 1921 to 13 October 1923) and then, later, the Buhagiar (14 October 1923 to 17 September 1924) Administrations[3] from the start, it often had

---

[1] Ċ. Bugeja, 'For a Labour Programme'.
[2] Bonnici, 87.
[3] From 14th October 1923, the General Committee of the party had accepted the coalition with the *Unionisti*; and were given two ministries: Col. William Savona became Minister of Post, while Mr. Dundon became Minister of Health. Bonnici, 59.

disagreements with the leftist elements in the Labour quarters. In many cases, the parliamentary group took decisions without consulting the Labour executive – contrary to what they were expected to do.

Some, on the left of the party, had believed in an intransigent ideological and tactical stand against any compromises with the parties representing the ruling landowning and clerico-professional classes. According to them, the party in government should not be given any support. Their most influential intellectual, Ċensu Bugeja, was of the opinion that

all bills tending to perpetuate the Capitalist system and the class state, however beneficial they may appear judged from the standpoint of the present regime, should not have one Labour vote in their support.[4]

Many members of the Labour general committee were in favour of the strict autonomy of the party. Indeed the left-wing elements, or 'Bugeja's section' as it was called in the Labour executive, continued to view this coalition as having been made in bad faith till its end.[5]

On 15 June 1924, the general committee of the Labour Party met, and Ġużè Orlando presented a motion to terminate the coalition in government. The general committee decided that the Labour Party should remain independent. On the other hand it was ready to help any party which would legislate the policies set out in the Labour Programme.[6] Later, on 12 October 1924, the general committee decided by 43 votes against 15, to stop backing the government. However the Labour members of Parliament, led by Canon Carmelo Bugelli and Salvu Zammit Hammet did not accept this decision. Later still in October 1924, William Savona, leader of the Labour Party, proposed a vote of no confidence in the government, which was saved by Bugelli's and Zammit Hammet's votes. The latter two were *ipso facto*

[4] Ċ. Bugeja, 'For a Labour Programme'.
[5] Ċ. Bugeja, 'Il Partit tal Haddiema u l Coalizioni'.
[6] Anon., *Il-Qawmien tal-Haddiem Malti*, 36.

The two sides of a fly-sheet promoting the Compact. This fly-sheet, dated 11th June 1927, was sponsored by Maltese emigrants in Detroit.

expelled from the party,[7] the coalition broke up and the national corporatist ideal of the political representatives of the ruling classes remained an unrealized dream. However, the Buhagiar administration, did not have to resign because of the continued support by Bugelli and Zammit Hammet.

Right from the foundation of the Labour Party, the main criticism by the Constitutional Party was levelled against the domination of the clerico-professional elements in the directorship. The Labour leadership was attacked as being unrepresentative of the workers and composed of the most conservative elements in society whose interests were actually

[7] Bonnici, 94.

antagonistic to those of the working classes.[8] The political
alternative formulated by the Constitutional Party was the
creation of some form of an alliance between the workers in the
Labour Party and the progressive elements of the middle classes
which were the backbone of the Constitutionalists. One must
remember that the latter party's supporters included also many
workers, particularly from the Dockyard and who were therefore
dependent upon the Colonial Authorities.

On 11 January 1924, Sir Gerald Strickland wrote to the
Labour executive to sound the possibility of a united front in
the legislative assembly.[9] However, the Labour Party was not
yet prepared to accept this invitation because the party was
undergoing a structural and ideological transformation. A
compromise of that sort would need a transformed progressive
Labour leadership, which would be acting out the role of a
political ally. While this process in the Labour Party was going
on, a future alliance between this party and the Constitutionals
could be expected.

Meanwhile the two parties representing the traditional
mercantile and clerico-professional classes (PPM and PDN) fused
into one entity forming the *Partito Nazionalista* with a
reactionary programme for the maintenance of the *status
quo*.[10] All this produced a strong anti-reformist movement
which could effectively obstruct any potential reformist force
that envisioned gaining power and transforming society
economically and socially. The Catholic Church itself was to be
the most important catalyst helping to weld together the various
parts of this reactionary block. This fusion was nothing but a
political manifestation of the social polarization which was fast
evolving.

[8] J. Pace, 'Il Professionisti fil Partit tal Haddiema', *Il Progress*, 21 March 1924.
[9] Anon., *Il-Qawmien tal-Ħaddiem Malti.*
[10] It had been known from October 1925 that the *UPM* and the *PDN* were
negotiating a complete fusion with the organization of the Nationalist Party.
This fusion came about in 1926. The *Direzione Suprema* of the fusion was in
the hands of a triumvirate: Dr Ugo Mifsud, Dr Enrico Mizzi and Count Caruana
Gatto. *In Nazzion*, 16 January 1926.

By 1925, the seventh executive of the Labour Party had already been given the responsibility of discussing all possibilities for an alliance with the Constitutional Party in order to counterbalance the strength of the new *Partito Nazionalista*.[11] The Labour Party underwent a great reorganization in these years, beginning in 1925 when it reshuffled its leadership and gave more power to the grassroot district committees. New personalities formed the leadership, and the party now began to be dominated by progressive and socialist elements.[12] With this change in structure and composition of the leadership, the ideological perspective of the Labour Party shifted towards socialism.

The assimilation of socialist, secular, and enlightened liberal ideas brought in by some of the new elements changed the ideological orientation in the party itself. The influence of Dimechianism (which, in itself, was an assimilation of ideological influences, intelligently adapted to the local situation), British socialism with its Protestant and liberal inheritence, and a tradition of Jacobin ideology, were assimilated subtly in the ideological formation of the main leftist exponents in the leadership.

According to the new leadership, the first means to step up their influence over the masses was to strive with every possible means to educate the workers towards their emancipation, making education the primary objective of the Labour intellectuals.[13] The Party's novel strategy was to help the Constitutional Party to gain power because of its greater numerical strength so that it would help to pass social legislation. Education, it was believed, eventually would lead the masses to support the Labour Party.[14]

Tactical considerations were now the main questions facing the new labour leadership:

[11] Bonnici, 99.
[12] See Table 1.
[13] P. Boffa, introduction to Bonnici.
[14] Ċ. Bugeja, 'Malta a Nation', *Labour Opinion*, 4 March 1926.

The more revolutionary position of the Labour programme should be kept in the background at first, unless, of course, the Labour Party is from the very start in a position to assume the reins of Government.[15]

From this leftist perspective, Strickland, a Conservative Party member in the British House of Lords, was considered to be a member of the wealthy classes, like the other privileged personalities forming part of the social élite. However, even though Strickland himself was a landowner, the party he led represented the interests of a potentially capitalist middle-class and not the traditional middle-class.[16] Labour had to differentiate between the wealthier classes, and grasp the opportunity offered by this class difference for bettering its own interest. According to Ċensu Bugeja, Strickland's government would have been the same as its predecessor (even though for other reasons), if Strickland's party succeeded to win the next elections by itself.[17] Strickland was considered a cunning politician (brikkun), but the Labour Party was to help him come to power and use him[18] to legislate in the interests of the working class.

A compact between the two parties was the best immediate formula which would express a basic class alliance and common inspirations. It was also the most advantageous tactical move which, according to Ċensu Bugeja, had to be skilfully steered to result in one of these alternatives:

If the parties with whom we make agreements keep their word, the working class electorate will know that it is through us that they have obtained beneficient legislation, and their future support is assured. If, on the other hand, the other parties abuse the confidence we repose in them, it will become clear to the workers that they can never obtain anything except from the party which professedly champions their cause.[19]

---

[15] Ċ. Bugeja, 'For a Labour Programme'.
[16] Ċ. Bugeja, 'L'Iscop tal partit tal Haddiema', *Labour Opinion,* 25 October 1923.
[17] *Ibid.*
[18] 'Conferenza l'Isla', *Labour Opinion,* 9 April 1925.
[19] Ċ. Bugeja, 'Malta a Nation'.

One of the several logos (by the caricaturist A. Gerada) used by the politico-satirical paper *Il Hmara*.

Negotiations started when, in 1925, the fusion of the PPM and the PDN was already becoming a reality. In fact, Carmnu Longo and Ġużè M. Grech from the Labour Party and three members from the Constitutional Party met privately and discussed the possibilities of a compact.[20] The Labour executive passed a resolution, suggested by Mosè Gatt, which declared that any invitation for a 'round-table' conference from any one party would be accepted.[21] Thereupon the Constitutional Party invited a Labour delegation to discuss the possibility of a compact.

On 1 December 1925, the Labour delegation reported to the executive on a proposed 'Draft Compact'.[22] The next day this draft was approved by the Labour general committee with 87 votes against 1, and 12 abstentions. On 25 January, in the Constitutional Club in Valletta, the Compact between the Labour and Constitutional Parties was signed.[23] In appendix A

[20] Bonnici, 100.
[21] *Ibid.*
[22] See Appendix B.
[23] Bonnici, 102.

of this Compact, the parties agreed to amend the electoral law, especially with regard to those who were illiterate and had no vote, and to give Maltese the status of an official language alongside English. The two parties agreed to combat unemployment and to give aid to those Maltese who were going to emigrate to countries in the empire. Point number six of this appendix was very important. It suggested the introduction of a Workmen's Compensation Act. Other major important points were the introduction of compulsory instruction and the building of schools. Technical education was to be encouraged. No taxes were to be imposed on imported industrial equipment and raw materials. Other suggestions in this Compact regarded the law of succession, the Trade Union Act and the building of a modern hospital for the poor. Amendments to the rent law and the building of more houses for the workers were also given consideration.[24] All these points were immediate objectives which the Compact parties agreed upon.

Such common objectives as technical education and the freeing of local industries from tax burdens on raw material and imported industrial equipment showed the Compact's main aspiration of industrializing the country. This was the basic issue of the alliance. Industrialization was viewed as the only means for progress. Even Manwel Dimech and his followers had viewed industrialization as the only solution to the misery of the population. Their major enemies were the traditional unproductive bourgeoisie, which they described as bigots without any social conscience and passive parasites without any initiative.[25] This ideological stand had other implications on society in general. The Compact's programme was aimed at reforming society by orienting the economy towards the manufacturing industry and export.

The traditional conservative mercantile, clerico-professional classes saw in the Compact, with its liberal enlightened ideas, secular outlook and modernizing vision of society, a threat to

---

[24] See Appendix B.
[25] M. Chetcuti, 'Iz zmien u il fkir ta Malta', *Il Fkir Malti* 27 September 1923.

their hegemony. The reformist movement was actually consolidated by the Compact which the political block of the right interpreted and represented as anti-Catholic, anti-clerical, and godless. It was also described as being composed of Jews and Protestants and of being a freemasons' plot.[26] However, this generic and propagandistic terminology exhibited by the anti-reformists is very interesting when analysing the essence of the Compact.

The Constitutional Party was the political representative of the new middle-class which was composed of contractors, traders, pro-British importers, civil servants, employees in the civil administration,[27] and a handful of capitalists who were prepared to invest in manufacturing concerns. The strife for secularization and for the recognition of Maltese as the language of the people, the belief in parliamentary democracy and liberalism, and the emphasis on production rather than on consumption, were all characteristics of this new middle-class reformist ideology. This was an ideological inheritance of the Protestant ethic which helped to transform north European feudal societies into industrial capitalist ones.[28] This capitalist ethic which establishes capital increase as its ultimate point of reference,[29] was evident in many characteristics of the Maltese pro-British middle-class which looked at the future in a progressive way:

On the one hand the entrepreneur is unmistakably oriented toward the future, as is shown negatively by his abstention from present consumption and by the willingness to ignore and violate tradition and positively by his expectations of a long-run return from investment.[30]

[26] Mannarinu, 'Il Processioni Protestanta f'Malta u l'Istricklandjani', Il Ggant, 26 January 1929.
[27] E.L. Zammit, A Colonial Inheritance, 46.
[28] U. Carroni, 'Crisi ideale e transizione al socialismo', Critica Marxista, 41.
[29] G. Poggi, Calvinism and the Capitalist State – Max Weber's Protestant Ethic, 46.
[30] G. Poggi, 43.

However, as has happened in other Latin countries, the local new middle-class, was not actually able

to fulfil a historical role as the carrier of a bourgeois revolution, generating its own values and stimulating economic developments'.[31]

The small new middle-class was not strong enough and had to depend on the numerical strength of the Labour members in the Compact. In fact, the composition of this new middle-class was ambiguous, and this was the main reason for its weakness. The number of potential industrialists, whose capitalist spirit was developed to the point of risking their relatively limited capital in the manufacturing industry and export, was small.

In theory, the reformist movement's directorship envisaged an industrialized export-oriented economy, but the raw material, and the necessary dynamics for such a process were extremely scarce. The Compact, therefore depended on the goodwill of the working classes and the patronage of the British authorities, for its survival. This reformist alliance, in order to function, had to be cemented by a populist praxis which was naturally also reflected in the Compact's ideology. In fact, populism has been described as the result of a situation in a particular country at a particular time where the middle classes were too weak and heterogeneous to affirm their hegemony and ideological control over society.[32]

The heterogeneous nature of the small and weak new middle-class in Malta, had to be sustained in the Compact with a charismatic leadership which could hold the movement together. The populist leader, moreover, had also to be a mediator who, by means of patronage, could integrate the new social forces with the established political system. In fact, Strickland was to prove instrumental in the integration of the reformist movement. He was a clear example of a charismatic populist leader, alike others in similar historical situations, whose functions of patron and broker,[33] clearly stood out.

---

[31] A.E. Van Niekerk, *Populism and Political Development in Latin America*, 26.
[32] *Ibid.*
[33] A.E. Van Niekerk, 180.

Protestant nonconformism had played an important role in the origins of the Labour movement in Great Britain, which in turn also influenced the Labour Party in Malta. This type of nonconformism helped to bring the Compact parties closer together, as both shared, to some extent, this ideological heritage. The AMILP, a branch of the British Independent Labour Party, had been a staunch exponent of working-class nonconformism, but it was numerically very small and its influence limited.[34] However, many ex-AMILP members joined the Compact, and Carmelo Zammit, for example, became one of its most prominent defenders and exponents.

This reformist/anti-conformist ethic in the new middle-class is seen also in the latter's antagonism towards the Catholic Church. It came quite naturally as it had to combat the deeply-rooted feudal remnants of the landowning class and the

GIUZÈ ORLANDO   Censu Bugeja

Giuzè Orlando and Censu Bugeja as depicted by caricaturist Gerada.

[34] 'The Anglo-Maltese Independent Labour Party', *supra* vide *Chap.2*

hegemony of the hierarchical Catholic Church over the people. The whole compactist movement manifested this kind of reformist heresy in its ideology. Anti-clerical incidents were frequent, and mostly came from the Constitutional quarters. A case in point was when *Il Progress,* the organ of the Constitutionalists, offered prize money to whoever gave the best reason why the old Bishop of Gozo should resign.[35] The Compact activists got into trouble with the local clerical authorities on several occasions, the most notable events being the Pentecost demonstration in St John's Co-Cathedral[36] and the *Viva Calles* incident in July 1928.[37]

It was natural that the Compact should immediately clash with the Catholic Church in a complicated religio-political dispute. This was almost inevitable in a society dominated by Catholicism in all its spheres. Education, law, philosophy, morality and philanthropy, were all under the Church's control. The local Church, like its counterpart in Latin countries was also an instituted landowning force. The ecclesiastics were the people's intellectuals, organically linked to the landed aristocracy.[38] In time it had assimilated in its ranks many respected and intelligent members of society. Ċensu Bugeja had feared, and warned about, the possibility of a fusion of all the anti-reformist forces, because he justly believed that, the church and the two parties (the PDN and the PPM) represented common interests in society.[39]. The organic bond of the ecclesiastics, the landowners and the professional classes made the priests the most fervent exponents of this reactionary block. So it is not surprising to find prominent priests, like Father Anton Tonna Barthet OSA, writing in 1927, telling the workers to serve their masters quietly and honestly and to abandon those who were

---

[35] *Il Progress,* 21 October 1921.
[36] Anon., 'The attacks on the Clergy', *The Daily Malta Chronicle,* 20 July 1928.
[37] See Circular 217 issued by the Archbishop of Malta deploring the latter incidents. *Il Habib,* 31 July 1928.
[38] A. Gramsci, *Selections from the Prison Notebooks,* 7.
[39] Ċ. Bugeja, 'Il Haddiem u l Costituzjonali, *Il Hmar,* 10 February 1926.

preaching socialism because this was an anti-Christian belief.[40]

This alliance of the ruling landowning clerico-professional classes and the local Church, created a block which manifested fascist tendencies. A *fascio* was opened in Valletta, and its activities were reportedly attended by leading personalities.[41] In their yearly calendar of events they celebrated amongst other occurances, the anniversary of the *Marcia su Roma*.[42] Fascist influence grew in the country as Mussolini looked on the island as *terra irredenta*. According to Count Ciano, the Italian Fascist Party provided financial aid to the Nationalists headed by Enrico Mizzi.[43] This block was essentially reactionary, strongly opposed to reformism, which meant the loss of the traditional ruling classes social hegemony over the populace. The Compact was seen as the antithesis of everything which Latin culture represented. This was manifested in a glaringly clear and significant article in the Nationalist party organ, *Malta*. This article was intended as a theoretical justification of Fascism, which was seen as the culmination of reaction against all the enlightened trends originating in the Protestant reformation and developing into individualistic rationalism. Accordingly, Fascism was the culmination of a whole Latin civilization, and it was the bulkwark against all the rationalistic and individualistic tendencies rooted in the Reformation and developed by the Anglo-Saxons. Protestant, liberal, and Marxist movements were accordingly, all branches of the main current, inheriting the anti-Catholicism of the French Revolution. The modern liberal, socialist or communist theories were the latest descendants of this line of thought:

---

[40] A. Tonna Barthet, *Iz-Zerriegha l-Hazina*, 13: '*U intchom, haddiema, tingannaux lil padruni taghcom. Servuhom fedelment u tatux widen lil dauc li iridu igibu discordia u l'odiu contra Cristu, min hu contra u jahdem contra Cristu icun jahdem contra l'interessi taghcom.*
Haddiema ahdmu ghal Cristu u b'ecc tcunu tahdmu ghall'interessi taghcom u ticunu sigur felici.' [And you, workers, deceive not your masters. Serve them faithfully and heed not those who would sow discord and hatred of Christ, he who is against, and works against, Christ works against your interests.
Workers, labour for Christ and in this way you will be working for your own interests and you will certainly be content.]
[41] *Malta*, 25 July 1928.
[42] *Malta*, 24 October 1928.
[43] G. Ciano, *Diario 1937-38*, 234.

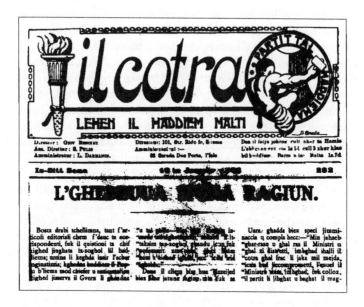

This conducting wire is the individualistic principle which is opposed to the Universal right of Rome.

Rousseau, the invisible leader of the French Revolution, and Marx, the creator of the First International, are on the same ideological level and are equally the product of the Reformation. Fascism, therefore, which is the antithesis of '89, is equally the antithesis of the Reformation; it is a return to the Universal right of Rome, of which the Catholic Church was the Saviour, the depository and the interpreter; and therefore... a return to the faith of our fathers, pure and granitic.'[44]

The reformist movement represented politically in the Compact was seen in the above ideological light, as an antithesis of all traditional beliefs. It was not only considered diametrically

[44] F.C., 'The Antithesis of the Reformation', *Malta*, 13 November 1928.

opposed to Fascism, but also to Catholicism and all that Latin culture stood for.

As the time for the elections approached in mid-1927, the Church did not take an open political stand against the Compact parties but the majority of the clerics made anti-reformist propaganda. The campaign led by prominent leaders of the ruling classes and the church depicted the Compact as a Protestant, Bolshevik, masonic alliance working to destroy Catholicism in Malta. It reached its climax with the distribution of a sworn affidavit against Strickland in which he was accused of being a freemason.[45] The elections for the *Assemblea Legislattiva* were held in August 1927, with these results:[46]

	Votes	%
Constitutional Party	14,130	41.0%
Partito Nazionalista/Ind.	15,079	43.8%
Labour Party	4,773	13.9%
Others/PNM	462	1.3%

The Compact had won, but the Labour Party had lost ground gaining only three seats in the legislative assembly and none in the senate. The Compactist front gained power under the leadership of Sir Gerald Strickland and distinguished itself with social legislation in the legislative assembly. In 1927, the Workmen's Dwelling Fund Act,[47] the Widows' and Orphans' Pension Act,[48] and the Workmen's Compensation Act[49] all successfully passed through both chambers. These were the concrete results of the Compact which, against enormous

[45] *Strickland Mazun ?!,*
[46] M.J. Schiavone, 41.
[47] *MGG,* 22 March 1927.
[48] *MGG,* 23 June 1927.
[49] *MGG,* 29 April 1929.

opposition, succeeded in legally working out certain rudimentary and basic reforms in society. The Compact was also a political instrument by which a section of the new middle-class gained administrative power in the legislative assembly for the first time, with the backing of the working classes.[50]

Strickland Mazun ?!?

Jena haun taht iffirmat Ettore Bono niddichiara li meta Strickland chien Segretarin, geit mlith min Spiru Cilia, illum mejjet biex immur inservi phala waiter FIL-LOGGIA TAL MAZUNI li chienet tesisti fin-nnuru 27 Strada Stretta, il Belt. Il giurnata chienet ta Hamis ic-Circa, leiliet il Gimgha il Chira. Jena niftacar illi dic il-leila flimchien ma iehor Malti, li ma hemmx bzou iusemmu, ma Colonel Hughes Hallett, ma Admiral Hughes Hallet, Colonel Bridgeman A.O.C., u Doctor Martin u il Conslu American ta dac iz-zmien li ma niftacatcx x'chien jismu imma chien jokod Strada Mezzodi, **chien hemm† presenti anchi il Conti Strickland liebes bil fardal u l'armar tal mazuni**. Felic l'occasioni camrieri Maltin conna hamsa, u jena kabel mort hatt parir min ghand il Confessur tighi Padre Pupul Galea, li chien kulli nista inmur phula xghol, imma biss, ech uara xi hagia **ma** niehux scandlu.

ETTORE BONO

Declared Signed and Sworn to by the said Ettore Bono at Valletta, Malta this 6th day of August 1927. before me.

(Signed) V. FRENDO AZOPARDI

Public Prosecutor and Commissioner of Oaths.

TRADUZIONI

—   *Dika iddichiarazioni giet maghmula, iffirmata u mahlufa min Ettore Bono, il Belt Malta dina il giurnata is6 ta Auissu 1927 kuddiemi.*

(firmat) V. FRENDO AZOPARDI.

Prosecutur Pubblicu u Commissariu tal Giuramenti.

Mercurius Press.

The well-known affidavit in the form of a fly-sheet(distributed on the eve of the 1927 General Elections), by which Gerald Strickland was accused of being a freemason.

[50] Ċ. Bugeja, 'Malta Nazion': *'Hia tfisser, jew għanda tfisser id dhul definit tal 'Baxxi', cliem ghaziz ghal pseudo-Nazionalisti, bhala unitajit li jiffunzionau fl'organismu nazionali'. [It means, or should mean, the definite introduction of the 'Lower Classes', a phrase dear to the hearts of the pseudo-Nationalists, as units functioning in the national organism.]*

4

A Socialist Orientation

The pre-Compact reorganization of the Labour Party in 1925 resulted in a change in the party's official organ. In November 1925 the new secretary, Ġużè Orlando, suggested that the title of the party's journal, *Labour Opinion,* be changed to one in Maltese, in order to boost its sales, as it was in grave financial difficulties.[1] It was decided that *Labour Opinion* be published occasionally and distributed free with the Maltese language paper, *Il Cotra.* What actually happened was that *Labour Opinion* ceased publication with its one hundred-and-eightieth issue, on 24 June 1926. *Il Cotra* took its place on 1st July 1926.[2]

The changes in the directorship of the party's organ — its ideological orientation, style and language — reflected the shift of the leadership to the left. The new leadership concentrated more on communicating with the grassroots, the party's real

[1] Bonnici, 102.
[2] *Ibid.*

base of support. An ideological transformation can be confirmed from the articles which began to appear in the party's papers and other periodicals. Some articles in *Il Cotra* had an explicit Marxist tinge. Instead of the nationalistic and parochial utterances which had previously been the main issues, socialist internationalism began to be openly propagated. An article in *Il Cotra* for example, commented that the strength of the workers' movement lay in its internationalist character, a fact which some were beginning to understand.[3] The following extract clearly manifests the ideological orientation of the party's official organ:

Presently the British Crown, that is surrounded by many capitalists and led by a Conservative government, is in agreement with all other crowns and has no fear of being attacked. So, in peace time it economises and begins throwing out of work and forcing compulsory leave on the workers and the poor.[4]

Socialist influence can clearly be discerned in numerous other writings. The French Revolution as well as the Russian Revolution were treated in a sympathetic way. These revolutions were presented as the foundation of their movement's strength with the people revolting against different systems of oppression.

Significantly the writers who contributed to the first issues of *Il Cotra* were predominantly leftist. Their articles explicitly showed their ideological stand.[5] The pages of *Il Cotra* are full of prominent leftist names: Ġużè Ellul, Ġianni Gatt, John F. Marks, Wiġi Azzopardi, Ġużè Attard Bezzina, Salvu Pulis, Francesco Chetcuti, Joseph Grech (from Detroit, USA), Alfred

---

[3] U. Bonnici, 'Tolle Legge!...Tolle Legge!!', *Il Cotra*, 15 July 1926.
[4] F. Chetcuti, 'Il Guerer', *Il Cotra*, 26 July 1926.
[5] An article written by F. Chetcuti, a prominent Dimechian and socialist, began: 'Narau immela l'odju li jeżisti haun Malta, u narau mill liema classi gej hecc hux gej mill classi Proletaria (bhal ma keghdin ighejdu is skjavi) jew mill classi borghesa. [Let us see therefore the hatred that exists here in Malta, and let us see from which class it originates, whether it originates from the Proletarian class (as the lowers claim) or whether it is coming from the bourgeoisie.] 'L'Odio di Classe', *Il Cotra*, 14 October 1926.

Nicholas (from Cairo, Egypt), Pawlu Laus, Ġino Muscat Azzopardi, Charles Dougal, Wenzu Bonnici, Ġużè Micallef, Ġużè Orlando, Nazzareno Carabott, and Salvu Zammit.

Most of these contributors were either active *Dimechians* and/or members of the newly-formed Proletarian League. Salvu Zammit had been the secretary of the small AMILP.[6] Significantly in 1925 (VII Labour Executive) the editor of the party's organ became an official in the Labour executive for the first time. This was Ġino Muscat Azzopardi who remained in charge of *Il Cotra* until 1929. Ġużè Ellul Mercer filled in this post in 1930.[7] This shifting of *Il Cotra's* directorship to the left secured the ideological orientation of the Labour Party.

In 1926 socialist and revolutionary elements coordinated their efforts to form the *Ghakda Proletaria Maltia* (Maltese Proletarian League). A number of those active in the Labour Party, including some of the prolific contributors to *Il Cotra*, became members of this society. A few of them, such as Salvu Pulis and Wiġi Azzopardi became prominent activists. Others including Ġino Muscat Azzopardi, Ġużè Orlando, Ġużè Ellul, Frans Chetcuti, John F. Marks and Ġużè Gatt maintained very good ties with the League till its end.

In October 1926, the Proletarian League published a pamphlet entitled *L'Idea Socialista*.[8] Some weeks before, John F. Marks had written on the front page of *Il Cotra* that a pamphlet on socialism was about to be published, and that it was written by one 'whom we think is a friend of ours'. He recommended it to all workers in the country and wished success to its publishers.[9] Ġanni Gatt later an GhSM activist, welcomed this first publication on socialism in Maltese, and wished the new socialist society *ad multos annos*. He wrote that in Malta, where people did not know what socialism meant, such a pamphlet was

[6] see 'The Anglo-Maltese Independent Labour Party', Chap. 2.
[7] See Table 1.
[8] Anon., *L'Idea Socialista*.
[9] J.F. Marks, 'Spigulaturi', *Il Cotra* 16 September 1926.

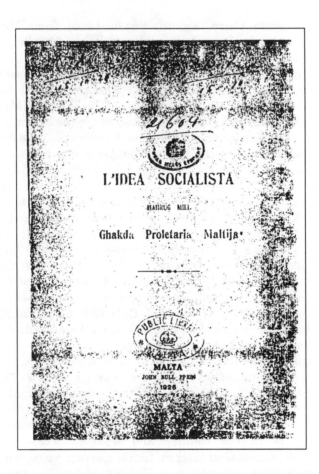

a necessary step in the right direction.[10] This review disturbed
some surviving conservative elements in the Labour Party.
Alfons Maria Galea protested to some members of the party's
executive against the publishing of such articles promoting a
socialist society.[11]

[10] G. Gatt, 'L'Idea Socialista', *Il Cotra* 14 October 1926.
[11] A.M. Galea, 'X'kitbulna', *Il Cotra*, 8 November 1926.

L'Idea Socialista included chapters on slavery, humanitarian thinkers, the French Revolution, progress, the International, the eight-hour work day, the First of May, the socialist movement, women, and education.[12] On the first page, the publication contained the Proletarian League Manifesto ('Our Mission'), which declared that workers had nothing to lose and that the League's mission was to educate the Maltese workers in an ideology (socialism) which as yet they had failed to understand. The League's aims were to instruct the proletariat by publishing socialist literature and to free the worker from mental slavery, so that he would build a strong socialist movement.[13] This pamphlet was financed by the League's members themselves, and any profit was to be used for the publication of other booklets.[14] The objective of the first booklet was to give the readers the basic theoretical concepts of socialism, and propagate its ideals among the workers:

Haddiema! meta takrau dan il ctieb, uara hemm bzon id-dahlu f'kalbchom; l'ideal, il fidi; is-socialismu u tcunu convinti minnu li hua veru taghlim ghal helsien taghna il haddiema; u ma inhallu katt lill partiti l'ohra idauruna ghal cull ma ighajdu u ifixclu biex jifirduna minn xulxin...
      Haddiema! Ninghakdu ilcoll, ahna m'ghandna xejn xnitilfu hlief il jasar economicu u sociali taghna!...
      Viva is socialismu il helsien taghna il haddiema![15]

[Workers! after you read this book you should instil the ideal, the creed of socialism in your hearts and be convinced that it is the true teaching for the freedom of us workers. Let us never permit the other parties

---

[12] Anon., *L'Idea Socialista*.
[13] Anon., 'Il Missioni Taghna', *L'Idea Socialista* : *'biex nuru lill classi tas sinjuri u tal professionisti_li li stess haddiema keghdin jiehdu sihem biex ikanklu il moviment tax-xoghol u tal haddiema, li sallum iridu izommulu il menti tighu ilsira dauc it-taparsi patriotti taht madmad u mantell tal ipocresia.'* [so as to show the monied and the professional class that the very workers are taking part to set in motion the labour movement, the worker's movement, that movement whose mind, those pseudo-patriots, labouring under the yoke and mantel of hypocricy, till this very day, want to hold in servitude.]
[14] *Ibid.*
[15] Anon., *L'Idea Socialista*, 20.

to make us believe all they say, to confuse and divide us...
Workers! Let us all unite; we have nothing to lose but our economic
and social serfdom...
Long live socialism and the freedom of us workers!]

They knew that the reactionary forces would attack them by
a thousand means and distract the workers.[16] However, the
first booklet was a success, as it sold over 900 copies,[17] mostly
in the Dockyard. Its influence would be felt in the immediate
future.

However on 3 November of the same year a circular, numbered
178, and signed by Rev. Canon Salv Camilleri was issued by
the Archbishop's Curia. In it, the archbishop 'in order to put
the people on their guard' condemned *L'Idea Socialista* as
gravely dangerous.[18] The Archbishop asserted that the social
question was not, as the socialists said, a purely economic
matter, but was overwhelmingly a moral one. The circular went
on to say that the Archbishop was very surprised when *Il Cotra*
reviewed the pamphlet and wished the society a long life, and
it concluded by condemning the pamphlet and instructed all the
faithful not to read it.[19] Mgr. Michael Gonzi, Bishop of Gozo,
also issued a Pastoral Letter, which described the pamphlet as
a venomous instrument with 'words of fire'.[20] So great was the
revulsion to Mgr. Gonzi's words that only some days after the
pastoral letter was read out the *Ghakda Proletaria Maltia*
declared itself disbanded. The declaration released by the
League and published in *Il Cotra* said that the Proletarian

---

[16] *Ibid.*
[17] (Law Court Archives, Valletta,) S(edition) T(rial 1933), 231.
[18] The Circular's essence could be read from this extract: *'alle idee e concetti
pescati da publicazioni certamente non Cattoliche, si predica l'ugualianza di
tutti, si fomenta l'odio di classe, si distrugge l'amore della Patria, si cerca di
insinuare nella mente dell'operaio Maltese che una classe di persone cerca di
tenerla nell'ignoranza, dichiarando in fine il socialismo internazionale giusto
come il Cristianesimo.'* Circolare 178, 3 November 1926, in Mintoff, 'Journalism
in Malta', 567.
[19] *'Pertanto, con' la presente circolare condaniamo l'opuscolo in parola a tutti
i fedeli di questa diocesi la lettura.'* Ibid..
[20] Anon., 'Il pastorali ta' l'Iskof ta' Ghaudex', *Il Habib,* 15 November 1926.

League had no intention of agitating an uprising and even less of attacking the Catholic Religion.[21] For the moment, the first outright socialist organization born out of the best intellectuals of the proletarian class, with a distinctive ideological bearing, had seemingly been dispersed. However, time would demonstrate that this was not the case.

The Emergence of a Proletarian Organization

On 6 March 1927, five months after the censure of the archbishop, some of the founding members of the Proletarian League, incorporated this supposedly defunct association into the *Ghakda Socialista Maltija*, (GhSM). *[Maltese Socialist League]*[22] The latter's first appearance was marked by a new publication in Maltese, the booklet, *Lill Haddiema*, which was published a year after the condemnation of *L'Idea Socialista*. The GhSM could not find any printer to take the job and the society's members had to buy a small printing press which they named *L'Internazionali*. The booklet was financed by the members themselves,[23] and it was a success for the *Ghakda Socialista Maltija* as it sold most satisfactorily, in spite of continuous attacks by the Catholic papers.

All registers and documents of the Proletarian League were continued by the new socialist society.[24] This proved that the only thing which had changed was the name, but this change in name brought about the enrolment of new members.[25] However, after some time, a most important amendment changed the statute of the *Ghakda Socialista Maltija*. The first section, which had declared the main principles of the society

[21] *GH.P.M.*, 'Dichiarazioni', *Il Cotra,* 11 November 1926.
[22] Homo, *Il Haddiem*, Malta, 1927, 20.
[23] *Ibid.*
[24] *S.T.* evidence of U. Azzopardi, p.563.
[25] *Ibid.*

to be based on those of the Independent Labour Party,[26] was changed to affirm that they were now those of International Socialism.[27]

One of the immediate aims of some members in the Proletarian League had been that of attracting with their 'redness' the attention of the periodicals and newspapers which were against Labour and the Compact, and to give to the Labour Party an open field to fight the 1927 elections.[28]

Ġużè Flores, Salvu Pulis,[29] and Salvu Delicata, who was secretary at the time,[30] were three of the founding members.

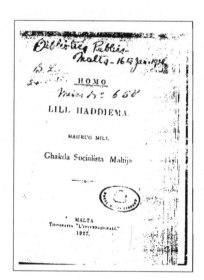

[26] *S.T.* evidence of S. Pulis, 623.
[27] *Ibid.*
[28] *Ibid,* evidence of U. Azzopardi, 563.
[29] *Ibid,* evidence of S. Pulis, 614.
[30] *Ibid,* evidence of C. Carabott, 441

Other members included Saverio Delicata who later emigrated to Tunisia, though he remained a prominent member of the *Ghakda Socialista Maltija* till 1929. Wiġi Azzopardi, who was to make a name in the movement's left, was also a very prolific writer in *Il Cotra*. He later contested the general elections as a Labour candidate. He had been invited from the beginning to join the *Ghakda Proletaria*, but had not accepted.[31]

He later declared that he had joined on the assurance by Ġużè Flores that the new association was to be different from the first. One of the most ideologically-advanced members was undoubtedly Salvu Pulis, who remained active till its end.[32] Pulis had also been a member of Dimech's *Xirka tal-Imdawlin [League of the Enlightened]* and remained an ardent socialist and Dimechian throughout his life.

Dimechian Roots

Many individuals with Dimechian connections, or who had been with Dimech, had from the start joined the Maltese Socialist League (GhSM).[33] In fact the new association was, from its beginning, accused of being Dimechian, and of looking at Manuel Dimech (who by then had obtained a notorious reputation with the social élite) as the first Maltese socialist martyr.[34] One of the reasons why the Nationalist party organ *Malta* reacted so strongly against the new society was the latter's declared political tendencies inspired by Dimechianism.[35] Furthermore, one of Dimech's daughters was also, allegedly, a member of the League.[36] Dimechian influence

---

[31] *Ibid,* evidence of U. Azzopardi, 563.

[32] *Ibid,* evidence of S. Pulis, 614.

[33] Some of these elements formed the Labour left, and were considered to be outspoken and fearless. This wing, knowing that the Church is rich in land it begins by wanting its' land, sees that priests are exempt from the burden of having to rear families and it attacks priests. [Seven Wise Men], [Divisions in the Labour Party.]

[34] Anon., 'X'inhu s-Socialismu', *Militia Christi*, September 1928.

[35] Catholicus Romanus, 'La propaganda anticlericale degli Stricklandiani' *Malta*, 16 August 1928.

[36] *S.T.* 245.

on the Maltese Socialist League was evident in many ways. For instance Salvu Delicata in an important letter to Carmelo Carabott, stated that the emancipation of the lower classes in Malta was primarily due to Manuel Dimech and then to the *Ghakda Socialista Maltija*:

Curagg, gia li il-lum zmien id-daul u causa ta id-daul f'Malta chien l-euuel Dimech imbaghad l-Ghakda. Dac harat u ahna zraina u nibet ghax f'art tajba.[37]

[Courage, today is the age of enlightenment and the cause of this light in Malta, was first Dimech and then the League. The former ploughed, we sowed, and it sprouted, because the soil was fertile.]

The Socialist League was considered the direct descendant of *Dimech's Xirca tal Imdauulin [League of the Enlightened]*. In fact, the Socialist League had set out as its main aim to strive for a republic – even though in a socialist rather than a Jacobin sense. Dimech himself had made it a rule for every member of the *Xirca* to adhere to Internationalism. He had also written on socialism on many occasions in his paper *Il Bandiera tal Maltin*. Socialism for Dimech was an anti-militaristic ideology, the source of hope for those living in misery and under any kind of tyranny; it was a belief based on the principles of universal brotherhood and peace.[38] The internationalist character of socialism with its great emphasis on anti-militarism was also greatly emphasized by socialist publications. A perfect example is a book by a prominent Socialist League personality, Duminku Degiorgio, *Il Gwerra tad dinja jew l'ikbar omicidju kollettiv*, deals with the problems of peace, militarism and war. This book

---

[37] *Ibid.*, 242, 'Curagg, gia li il-lum zmien id-daul u causa ta id-daul f'Malta chien l-ewwel Dimech imbaghad l-Ghakda. Dac harat u ahna zrajna u nibet ghax f'art tajba. Issa ghad irid jigi zmien ilhsad (it-trionf tas-socialismu) u jekk ma incunux iz-zazah tal lum icun ta zmien actar civilizzat.' [Courage, today is the age of enlightenment, and the cause of this light, in Malta, was first Dimech and then the League. The former ploughed, we sowed and it sprouted because the land is fertile. Now harvest time has yet to come (the triumph of socialism) and if it is not us, the present young generation, it will be that of a more civilized age.]

[38] M. Dimech, 'Sena Hsieb – Awissu 1914', in G. Azzopardi, *Ghejdut Manwel Dimech*, 40.

was published in 1939 just before the outbreak of the Second World War.[39]

One main reason for the influence of Dimechianism on the members of the Socialist League was that copies of Dimech's publications were still in circulation. For instance, copies of *Il Bandiera tal Maltin* were found in Ġanni Valvo's possession in 1933[40] at a time when Dimech's works were still considered incriminating.[41] Valvo also held in his possession Dimech's photograph,[42] which was deemed seditious material. Everything, in fact, which was in any way related to Manwel Dimech, was considered incriminating by the authorities. On the other hand Dimech was the hero most admired by the Socialist League members and by all those on the left. The League was later to circulate and sell copies of Manwel Dimech's photograph.[43] The Socialist League committee even decided — and unanimously agreed[44] — to begin investigating the possibility of publishing Dimech's work *Maisi Cutajar* or *It Tesor tal Palazz tal'Inquisitur*. Nothing ever materialized however.

[39] D. Degiorgio, *Il Gwerra tad-Dinja jew l-Akbar Omicidju Kollettiv.*
[40] *S.T.,*264.
[41] *Ibid.*
[42] *Ibid.,* 78
[43] This photograph was advertised in the Socialist League publications as follows: '*ITRATT tal Prof. E.Dimech — Li cull Malti specialment il haddiem ghandhom izommu fi djarhom bhala Proto Martri Socialista Malti.*', Anon., *X'Inhu s-Socialismu,* 1928, 23. [PHOTOGRAPH of Prof. E. Dimech — which every Maltese, especially the worker, should have in his home as the Maltese Socialist Proto Martyr.]
[44] *S.T.,* 243.

EMMANUEL DIMECH

5

The Sedition Trial and the End of the Left

The Maltese Socialist League.

The Socialist League members were in the main dockyard workers.[1] This is borne out by the original name of the League, *Ghakda Proletaria Maltija* (Maltese Proletarian League). This purely proletarian society emerged from the dockyard where its day-to-day activities were confined.[2] The dockyard was the only large industrial complex on the island where the workers were class-conscious proletarians. The socialist activists were the most ideologically advanced elements of their class. They were, in a Gramscian sense, organic intellectuals of the working class.

The Socialist League on the other hand, was the result of a political development which had its roots in the experiences of past organizations and struggles. Dimechianism was one of the basic ideological tenets of the *Ghakda Socialista Maltija,*

[1] See list of *GH.S.M.* members, Appendix C.
[2] PAV Des. No. 60, Enclosure 11, Gov. David G.K. Campbell to S.S.C., P. Cuncliffe Lister, 3 April 1933.

(Maltese Socialist League) which was by now historically rooted
in the minds of the Dockyard workers. The Dockyard, in fact,
was always considered to be a hotbed of 'red' political activities.
Many workers from rural areas found in the Dockyard a political
school which oriented them to the left.[3] Socialist and
communist literature was always circulating clandestinely,
mainly distributed by the Socialist League members.[4]

Activists of the Socialist League such as Salvu Delicata, Nestu
Laiviera, Carmelo Carabott, Ġanni Valvo, Wiġi Azzopardi,
Francesco Pulis, Duminku Degiorgio, Mosè Gatt, Carmelo
Ritchie, George Vella, and others[5] were all Dockyard workers.
Many of their helpers and sympathizers among the labour
leadership, for example John F. Marks and Ġużè Orlando also
worked at the Dockyard. Only a few other prominent activists
in the Socialist League were not dockyard employees, such as
Salvu Pulis, who worked in a brewery, Ġużè Galea, a university
student, and Carmelo Demosani, a printer and President of the
Ghakda Stampaturi Maltin (Union of Maltese Printers).
Carmelo Ciantar, another prominent member of the Socialist
League, owned a small shop, with the name 'Arcades Hole' which
sold gramophones and records.[6]

Of significant importance is the relationship of the League's
members with the constituted political parties. Some socialist
activists were also members of either the Labour or the
Constitutional Party. As can be expected no member came from
the Nationalist Party. From 1926 onwards, the Labour Party
was always accused of being infiltrated by the Socialist League
members.[7] Indeed the Labour Party was challenged to publish
the names of its members who allegedly were also members of
the Socialist League.[8] The former's organ, *Il Cotra*, which was
attacked by the Church and the Nationalists as an extreme

---

[3] C. Carabott interviewed by the author, 7 January 1985.
[4] *Ibid.*
[5] See Appendix C.
[6] *Ibid.*
[7] S.T., 279
[8] *Id-dawl,* 27 November 1930.

radical and anticlerical periodical, was the rallying point of the left. Salvu Pulis wrote that *Il Cotra* was the true organ of the workers because it was of good ideological quality.[9] Not only the Socialist League members contributed to this newspaper but all leftist elements, including those prominent labour personalities who were always in contact with the League.

Significant too is the region that the members of the Socialist League came from. The great majority of the members originated from the Cottonera precinct. The greatest concentration was to be found in Senglea. The others came mostly from urban non-industrial areas such as the harbour area and other villages.[10] It was on the Senglea Labour Club, where John F. Marks was president, that the red flag was raised for the first time in 1926.[11] After this event it became normal for Labour clubs all over the island to raise the red flag.[12] Later that year, following a reorganization within the Labour Party, wherin the left had come out dominant,[13] the Senglea Labour Club[14] was to hoist another red banner – this time with the party's emblem in the centre. The Senglea club was the most active Labour district-branch, and had the largest concentration of radical elements.

The *Ghakda Socialista Maltija* officially adopted the plain red flag,[15] red being the colour of the international workers' movement. It was regarded as symbolic of the blood which unites all workers of the world into one movement.[16] The red flag began to be seen at every meeting, demonstration, political or social activity organized by the Compact. Furthermore, the Socialist League members and many in the Labour Party, especially in the Dockyard areas, used to sport red handkerchiefs. According to the socialists, the latter represented

---

[9] S. Pulis, 'Borg Gius P.L.', *Il Cotra,* 13 October 1927.
[10] See Table 2.
[11] S.T., evidence of P. Boffa, 438
[12] *Ibid.*
[13] *Ibid.*
[14] See Chapter 2.
[15] S. T. 279
[16] *Ibid.* 369

An advertisement of **Archades Hole** – the record-shop belonging to Carmelo
Ciantar – in *Il Kuddiem* of 1/1/1933.

a 'holy ideal' which materially and morally had to emancipate
the intellectual and manual workers from the low social and
economic position they were kept in.[17] The red handkerchief
was worn coming out from the left breast pocket of their
jackets.[18] Many socialists wore this in many a political
demonstration, a habit which became fashionable even with
some women.[19] From the beginning of the Compact, the red
flag and other such symbolism began to appear everywhere.[20]

[17] C. Grech, 'Il mactur ahmar', *Labour Opinion,* 4 November 1925.
[18] Id-Direzzjoni, 'Nota Stunata', *Lehen Is Sewwa,* 9 November 1929.
[19] Cetta il Bormlisa, 'L'Ahmar moda', *Il Hmara,* 24 July 1929.
[20] M. Scevola, 'Il Bandiera Hamra u l-Pulizija', *Internazionali?,* 17 December
1929.

Together with the red flag, the Socialist League had its own particular emblem. Salvu Delicata had designed one similar to that of Dimech's *Xirca*[21]. However this design was never presented to the Socialist League committee which then adopted the hammer and sickle. Salvu Pulis proposed adding the Marxist slogan 'Workers of the World Unite', but this proposal was not accepted.[22] The hammer and sickle (the design of which was taken from *La Rivoluzione Russa* published by Zanichelli of Bologna[23]) together with the Society's initials: *Gh S M*[24] were accepted by the committee.

The League was open to everybody who was a socialist, man or woman, whether living in Malta or abroad.[25] Every prospective member had to be approved by the committee. Afterwards, the President would call the new member and read to him the *Hsieb il Ghakda*, a sort of manifesto, and some other important chapters from the League's rules.[26] The new member would then sign a declaration in front of the President and the Secretary.[27] After declaring that he was a socialist and that he would work in the Socialist League, the new *Imsieheb (Comrade) would shake hands with the President and the Secretary as a sign that they would be* **shab fix-xoghol** (comrades in toil).[28] This meant that all members were to work for an International Socialist Republic and call each other comrade[29]. The initiation procedure served as a first means of organization and discipline and to bind the members closely together. Though the Socialist League was not strictly speaking a secret society, any member caught disclosing the names of other members was to be expelled.[30]

---

[21] S.T., evidence of S. Pulis, 452
[22] *Ibid.* 623
[23] *Ibid.* 614
[24] *Ibid.* evidence of C. Carabott, 452
[25] *GH.S.M.* Statute, Chapter 2, Article 2, S.T. 233.
[26] *GH.S.M.* Statute, Ch. 2, Art. 7; S.T. 234
[27] *GH.S.M.* Statute, Ch. 2, Art. 6; S.T. 234
[28] *GH.S.M.* Statute, Ch. 2, Art. 8; S.T., 234
[29] *GH.S.M.* Statute, Ch. 4, Art. 1, S.T., 233
[30] *GH.S.M.* Statute, Ch. 4, Art. 3, S.T., 238

One of the main objectives of the League was to spread International Socialist principles in Malta and abroad by means of printed material and any other form of propaganda.[31] This shows the importance propaganda was given by the League. An important section of the Statute stated that whenever the League published any literature, the committee members should be the first to sell it to the workers.[32] As the League could not finance the publication of its first book, the socialists decided to mete out the expenses themselves. The proceeds from this first publication would then be used to finance the second, and so on. Some other members not only helped to finance[33] the publication but also contributed towards the purchase of a small printing press which they named *L'Internazionali*. Carmelo Carabott, Duminku Degiorgio and Salvu Pulis worked on most of the booklets published by the League,[34] while many other members and sympathizers helped by sewing, stitching, pressing, correcting and proofreading these publications. This printing press was located in a stone hut near Corradino Prison at Paola.[35] The pamphlet *X'inhu Is-Socialismu*, which was

---

[31] *'L'GH.S.M. tuakkfet bil hsieb u r-rieda l'ix-xerred f'Malta u barra bil chitba u bil fomm it-tghalim Socialista scond il principii internazionali"* GH.S.M.Statute, Ch. 1, Art.1, S.T. 233.

[32] *GH.S.M. Statute, Ch.6, Art.13, S.T. 240.*

[33] Anon., *'Chelmtejn Taghna', X'inhu s-Socialismu.*

[34] C. Carabott interviewed by the author.

[35] J. Mamo gives a very detailed account of the place where the Socialists worked and printed their booklets and how they met and worked together. Here is an interesting extract:

'Cont tara, bhallichiecu, Duejra f'nofs ta ghalka bis sigar lejn Rahal Gdid kuddiem il Habs seuua; tidhol minn xatba, issib ruhec f'moghdija bil bajtar, tghauueg mal lemin u issib ruhec f'dahla bhal xekka tal Gharab. Imbaghad, geuuanett camra tauualija bla ebda nifs, mibnija bis sejjeh imcahhal. Stamperija ta cafcaf zghira, mixtrija bit-tkancic u 'l melh tal gharak. Cotba li jimleu il mohh imxerrdin l'haun u l'hemm fuk l'ixirca tal gebel; stampi ta nies cbar tax-xoghol maktughin minn xi magazines, xi wicc ta Tolstoi l'iwahhax, xi ihor ta Marx, xi Matteotti, xi Turati, xi Pasteur, xi ggant bil mazza f'idu, xi stampa ta' xi tkabida tan-nies tax-xoghol mal eghdewwa, xi bandiera hamra leun id-demm. Daun imwahhlin mal hajt bil colla, u hekk.'

J. Mamo, *Ulied in-Nanna Venut* 374-375.

probably written by John F. Marks, was printed there. Some
of the other publications in Maltese which were printed at the
Internazionali press were *L'Euuel ta Mejju* and *Il Faxxismu*,
both by S. Pulis (1929), and *Lill Haddiema* by Homo (1927).
Another publication was *Il Bandiera Hamra* (1928), one of a set
of fly-sheets which also included *L'Euuel ta Mejju*, *Infissru*, *Il
Poplu mahkur bi flusu*, and *Socialismu u Capitalismu*.

The Socialist League continued to print its own publications
during the first years of the Compact, that is until 1929, when
the politico-religious dispute led to the censuring of the
Constitutionalist and Labour newspapers by the archbishop.
From then onwards the printing press continued operating

clandestinely.[36] Many of the publications which the League issued were written by members of the League themselves. For instance, the first booklet, *L'Idea Socialista*, was written by Salvu Pulis, as were also the other two important pamphlets, *Il Faxxismu* and *Lill Haddiema*.[37] Duminku Degiorgio, a founding member of the League, later was to publish one of the most important books of the time, *Il Gwerra tad-Dinja jew l Ikbar Omicidju Kollettiv*. Wiġi Azzopardi also published *Il Fakar* in 1927[38] and was later to edit a socialist periodical entitled *Il Kuddiem ! Lehen il haddiem imcasbar*[39] published only four times in 1933. The latter three publications were printed in different printing presses and were not issued by the Socialist League.

The Socialist League propaganda did not only consist of printed matter in Maltese. The League, in fact, imported political literature of various kinds from different countries and sold or distributed them to the workers and members of the organization. The committee members corresponded with many foreign publishing houses, agencies, and individual publishers.

They received socialist and communist European reviews and journals such as *L'Humanité!, Daily Worker, Lo Stato Operaio, Avanti!,*[40] the anti-fascist organ *Liberta', Moscow News, Russia Today,* and the *Communist International*.[41] These were all widely read by the League's members who either subscribed to them individually, or bought them from Carabott's bookshop. The League corresponded through its secretary with other foreign organizations from whom a great deal of printed propaganda was obtained. It had started direct correspondence with the Rational Press Association, while Carmelo Carabott,

---

[36] C. Carabott, interviewed by the author.
[37] S.T. 403
[38] U. Azzopardi, *Il Fakar*
[39] U. Azzopardi published his address on every issue of this monthly journal which he directed (21, Sda, Reale, Casal Attard). The first issue of *Il Kuddiem Lehen il Haddiem Imcasbar,* was published on 1 January 1933.
[40] S.T. 410
[41] *Ibid.*, 66

secretary of the League, wrote to E.R. Pike of the same Association in London regularly.[42]

Other imported political literature included socialist almanacs such as the *Almanach d'Ouvriers et Paysans,*[43] and the *Almanacco Socialista* which was obtained in bulk by Ġużè Orlando from O. Morgari, the editor of the Italian Socialist organ *Avanti!*[44] Well known collections were also imported and sold by Carabott. These included the *Little Blue Books* edited by E. Holdman and the *Liberissima* collection which included a series of revolutionary writings such as *Riforma Fondiaria e Piccoli Coltivatori, La Libertà e la sua Guarantagie, Giuseppe Marinaro; una vita di lavoro e di Fede, La Rivoluzione Spagnola,* and *Un Socialista, Filippo Turati.*[45] This wide range of literature was imported by the League in accordance with its statute which allowed it to accept every kind of literature, "moderate or extremist".[46] A great quantity of Soviet revolutionary literature translated in English was also imported from such agencies as the *Kniga* in London.[47]

---

[42] C. Carabott, letter to E.R. Pike, The Rationalist Press Association Ltd., London, 30 March 1929, S.T. 41-43
[43] S.T. 410
[44] *Ibid.*, 329
[45] *Ibid.*, 38-39
[46] *GH.S.M.* Statute, Ch.6, Art.7, S.T., p.240.
[47] Some important literature from the above were:
V.M. Molotov, *The fulfilment of the first five year plan,*
M. Kaganovist, *The Socialist Reconstruction of Moscow,*
J.M. Gubkin, *The Natural Wealth of the Soviet Union and its exploration,*
V.M. Molotov, *The October Revolution and the Truth about Socialism, The Fundamental Law of the USSR (Constitution).*
Other classical socialist and communist literature were also imported and sold or circulated around. The list included such books and pamphlets as:
K. Marx, *Wage Labour and Capital.,*
K. Marx and F. Engels, *Manifesto of the Communist Party.,*
J. Reed, *10 Days that shock the world.,*
P. Kropotkin, *An Appeal to the Young.,*
Gorki, *Lenin.,*
G.B. Shaw, *Look you book.,* and
La Seconda Conferenza del Partito Comunista in Italia e la Seconda Conferenza dell C.G.C.T. (S.T. 37).

The International Class War Prisoners Aid,[48] (ICWPA) sent quantities of literature to the Socialist League which then sold or distributed them to its members. The *Ghakda Socialista Maltija* was an affiliated member of the ICWPA and correspondence between the two organizations was regular. In 1929, however, literature from this international organization, which was indirectly backed by the Comintern,[49] was being

---

[48] The International Class War Prisoners Aid (British Section) was organized in 1924, in order to aid victims of fascist oppression everywhere in the world but especially in countries such as Italy, Poland, Bulgaria, and in the British Colonies, Klugmann, vol.2, 81

[49] J. M. Ryle, 'International Red Aid and Comintern Strategy, 1922-1926' *International Review of Social History*.

confiscated by the British Authorities. This was happening all over the Empire. One of the letters sent by the ICWPA to Carmelo Carabott, dated 23 March, reads:

'Dear Comrade,
Very much thanks for your literature order of the 16th instant, which has been forwarded under separate cover today. Please let us know if you receive it safely, as, for some time now, much of our literature which we have sent to Malta, Canada, Australia, and New Zealand etc., has been confiscated by the Authorities.'[50]

This situation was later further complicated by the promulgation of the Governor's Ordinance XIX of 1932 which prohibited the importation of seditious literature.[51] Carabott, the Secretary of the Socialist League, wrote to all foreign associations and publishing agents who had contacts with the League to let them know about the situation, and suggesting that they wrap up all material posted to Malta in such a way as to make it difficult to identify.[52]

An Organized Left

As stated in the introduction, the 1921 constitution was a political compromise between the local privileged clerico-professional classes and the British colonial authorities. With the diarchical system of government, the British authorities secured jurisdiction over 'reserved matters' such as defence and foreign relations, while the local clerico-professional classes safeguarded their own interests and their control over great sections of society.[53]

The Compact between the Labour and the Constitutional Parties gained representative power in the 1927 general elections. However, as a reformist movement working within

---

[50] S.T. p.148
[51] *Ibid.*, 69
[52] C. Carabott's letter to the Worker's Bookshop Ltd., 3 October 1932, *S.T.* 147.
[53] See Introduction

the limits of the constitutional compromise of 1921, it found many legally defined boundaries which limited its objectives.

In carrying out social reforms through parliamentary legislation, the Compact was faced by a powerful Senate which obstructed moves for reforms passed by the Legislative Assembly. The leader of the Labour Party was later to state that:

The victory of the Constitutional and Labour Parties in 1927, was a source of some alarm to the old ruling class, but they began to get really preoccupied when the Compact government, obstructed by the Senate and encouraged by the campaign against the existence of the Upper House waged by the Labour Party from the very beginning of self-government, took steps to limit the powers of the Senate.[54]

The Labour Party took a clear-cut political position for the abolition of the Senate. It wanted to bring about fundamental changes in the 1921 constitution – a constitution which was the result of a compromise between the British colonial authorities and the clerico-professional classes and which had left out the working classes.

In the view of the MLP the constitutional changes required in order to avoid all possible causes which may develop into similar crises came under the following headings: a) The Senate
b) Language Question
c) Plural voting
d) Reserved matters.[55]

The Constitutional Party, faced by Labour's intransigent stand on the senate issue and by the working classes' hostility towards the senate, did nothing more than propose its mere reform.[56] Being in a very politically ambiguous position Strickland, as head of the Compact government, opted for a senate which would have all the characteristics of a house of review, like the House of Lords in Britain. However, Strickland declared that his party

---

[54] *Malta Royal Commission 1931*, evidence of Dr Boffa, 60-61.
[55] 'In these circumstances the M.L.P. is strongly of the opinion that the Senate should be totally abolished.' *Ibid.*
[56] *Daily Malta Chronicle*, 3 September 1928.

The workers' struggle against the Senate - a caricature by A. Gerada from
Il Felu, December 1928.

was contrary to the withdrawal of the senate and the 1921 constitution. He declared before the Royal Commission, that the Constitutionalists were completely against the reversion to Crown Colony government, but proposed changes in the 1921 constitution. These reforms included the securing of free elections; the removal of deficiencies which had appeared in the constitution; the reform of the senate; and the amendment of those sections in the constitution dealing with reserved matters in order to define more clearly the jurisdiction of the two spheres of the diarchy. The raising of Maltese to the status of an official language along with the development of the study of English was also suggested.[57] The Constitutional Party's position regarding the senate was greatly criticized by the Labour leadership and it seemed to be one of the main contentions and ever-pending issues within the Compact. For the Labour Party, the suggestion of the Constitutional Party was only a half measure:

It may give the Constitutional Party a chance to govern, but it will never do so for the Maltese Labour Party. The Constitutional Party might have the nobles with them, or if this political struggle between the Church and state be settled, they might have the priests with them; but the Labour Party will never have support from the Senate.[58]

The Constitutional Party's stand was fiercely criticized by the left within the Labour movement. Not only did socialist leaders in the Labour Party adopt an intrasigent stand against the senate, but they also wanted radical changes in the 1921 constitution.[59]

By criticizing the senate of a class division, the Socialist League worked for the total elimination of the senate together with the 1921 constitutional compromise, which it repudiated. One of the foremost intellectuals in the League, Wiġi Azzopardi,

---

[57] *Malta Royal Commission 1931,* evidence of Gerald Strickland, 3.
[58] *Ibid.,* evidence of Dr Boffa, 63
[59] *Ibid.*

highly criticized the Constitutionalists of being a bourgeois party. He stated that Strickland's party had betrayed the working class because it did not work in the latter's interests.[60] Azzopardi also wrote that the Constitutional Party was a party of opportunists because, when the issues involved touched its class interests, it had abandoned co-operation but it was in favour of the Compact when matters regarding social legislation were being dealt with.[61] Even Ġuże Orlando had written in his *Pamphlet tal Partit tal Haddiema* that the Compact was an 'unhappy marriage' between the two parties.[62]

The attack on the senate and the proposed changes in the 1921 constitutional compromise instilled fear in the rural landowners and the traditional privileged classes, for their own economic interests and social status were at stake.

The Nationalist Party was against any changes or reform of the 1921 constitution. Its leaders were against making any changes in the constitution unless they had the people's consent.[63] On its part the Church became the most important asset for the reactionary classes. It was diametrically opposed to everything the reformist movement meant and it was natural that it tried to present the Socialist League as a communist menace.[64] The church feared the propagation of revolutionary ideas and the League's growth into a political movement, as this would have meant an end to its own privileges. The reformist movement was also continuously attacked as being anti-clerical, Bolshevik and Protestant,[65] terms which were mainly used by *Leħen is-Sewwa*, the Church's official organ which commenced publication soon after the setting up of the *Ġjunta Djoċesana ta' l-Istampa t-Tajba*. The latter was established by an archbishop's pastoral, issued on 12 July 1928 concerning insults hurled at the senate and the church during a demonstration by

[60] U. Azzopardi, 'Il partit tal Haddiema', *Il Hmar*, 23 May 1928.
[61] U. Azzopardi, 'Nghamlu Compact jeu le?, *Il Hmara*, 25 January 1930.
[62] G. Orlando, *Pamphlet tal partit tal Haddiema*
[63] *Malta Royal Commission 1931*, evidence of Ugo Mifsud, 52.
[64] Catholicus Romanus, 'La Propaganda anticlericale degli Stricklandiani'.
[65] See issues of *Internazionali?* published in 1929.

MIZZI BROS. 'AUTOMOBILE DEALERS

THE SUN IX-XEMX

USAU DUNLOP TYRES L'ORHOS U L'AHJAR

No. 372   Stampat fill Progress   Malta, IS-SIBT, 21 TA DICEMBRU, 1929.   Jimbieh Sitt-habbiet

IL PERICLU TAL BOLXEVISMU F'MALTA.

The front page from an issue of **The Sun Ix-Xemx**; *a newspaper heralding the policies of the* Constitutional Party.

anticlerical Compactists. Cries of *Viva Calles* and *Abbasso Cristu Re* had been shouted out by demonstrators.[66]

In this way the Church fused much more tightly with the anti-reformist block on the eve of the planned 1930 elections and it most strongly opposed the Compact. The archbishop had already censured the Compact papers, *Ix Xemx, Il Hmar, Dr.Xecchec,* and *Il Progress.* On 1 May 1930, he issued a Pastoral which prohibited the electorate from voting for Strickland, or his party, or for those who had helped or supported him (the Labour Party.)[67]

The May Pastoral had repercussions not only on the voting decisions of the electorate, but also on the Labour Party itself[68] where the majority did not want to accept the conditions imposed by the archbishop in order to lift the censure from their party. Immediate elections for a new Labour executive brought those who were against a compromise with the archbishop once more to the leadership of the party. On the other hand the anti-Compactists were defeated.

William Savona resigned as President of the Labour Party and Dr Paul Boffa became leader. Carmelo Agius, Fr. Eġidio Galea Balzan, Ġużè Borg, Paul Demajo, and Ġużè Mifsud Ellul, led by Mikiel Caruana, left the Labour Party as they had not been elected to the executive. They formed a new party, *The Independent Labour Party* and Mikiel Caruana began publishing the new party's organ, *Id Dawl.*[69]

According to the Nationalists, the heightened politico-religious dispute had as its causes Strickland's anti-clerical policies and the Compact's attacks on the Church. However, to the Labour leaders, this dispute manifested other, deeper, roots:

---

[66] Ganado, 407.
[67] Koster, 112.
[68] Ganado, 419.
[69] Anon., *Il Qawmien tal-Ħaddiem Malti;* 66.

The root of the present trouble lies in the existence in Malta of a political class drawn mainly from the legal and clerical communities who, since the very beginning of British rule in Malta, held sway over the people in all matters.[70]

The Compact parties wanted to contest the elections — in spite of the Pastoral compulsion on the electorate — 'in order to end, once and for all, undue clerical influence in Malta'.[71] However, the British authorities suspended the elections and a provisional government was set up.[72] A Royal Commission was sent to analyse the political situation and to suggest recommendations. The commissioners' report recommended the restoration of parliamentary government which was 'to be elected in an atmosphere free from political bias'. However, intransigent elements in Britain commenting on the report of the Royal Commission opined that:

The essential result of their findings is that responsible government should forthwith be restored to the island, but they fail to produce any satisfactory evidence to show that the cause which brought about its suspension has been eradicated. They only say that after conversations with the Bishops they feel sure that any new pastoral which may be issued will differ from that of 1930, which rendered it impossible for the elections to take place. This is wholly inadequate, it in no way binds the bishops, still less the Holy See, and if as a matter of conscience the bishops feel bound to repeat even, less emphatically, their warnings of 1930, the result must be fatal to the Constitutional party. If the Government acts on the evidence now given, it is simply placing itself at the mercy of the bishops, who can perfectly justly say that they cannot be bound by any views of their intentions formed by the Commission or that the attitude of their opponents has forced them to alter their views.[73]

[70] *Malta Royal Commission 1931*, evidence of Dr Boffa, 60.
[71] Resolution by Compact parties as quoted in Borg, 46.
[72] *Ibid.*, 47
[73] *The Scotsman*, 13 February 1932.

The comment from *The Scotsman* (quoted above) seems to have been a prophecy because afterwards 'The Bishops saw the light and issued a fresh pastoral withdrawing the objectionable ones of 1930 and the previous month. The elections proceeded. Strickland was defeated and the so-called Nationalists returned.'[74] In fact, the May Pastoral was withdrawn but with the new Pastoral, the bishops reminded the population

to give their vote only to those candidates who may give sufficient guarantees that, so far as depends on them, there will be respected and conserved the religious interest of the Catholic people of Malta.[75]

Elections were held on the 11, 12 and 13 June 1932, and the results were: *Partito Nazionalista* 21 seats;
                   Constitutional Party 10 seats;
                   Labour Party 1 seat.[76]
With the return of the Nationalists to power by a great majority, the fear of the left that the people would put the local traditional ruling classes in parliamentary power because of clerical compulsion became real. The reformist movement of the Compact had been overwhelmed by the anti-reformist block led by the Nationalists and the Catholic Church. The pro-Italian trends of the latter, together with irredentist and anti-reformist forces had gained the upper hand. The local fascists emerged in the open and fascist propaganda grew.[77] In the regional context the Italian Fascist government was taking advantage of the opportunities created by the Maltese political situation:

Mussolini was not slow to take advantage of the situation. Doubtless the ambitions, which later exhibited themselves in the bombastic boasts that the Mediterranean would be the *Mare Nostrum*, were already simmering up and Malta was a formidable obstacle for the realization of that dream. No money was spared on Italian propaganda and

---

[74] Swinton, 90.
[75] *Lehen is-Sewwa*, 4 June 1932.
[76] M. Schiavone, *L'Elezzjonijiet f'Malta 1849-1981*, 47.
[77] Anon., 'La Casa del Fascio u 'l Casini tal Compact', *Id-Dehen*, 28 February 1931.

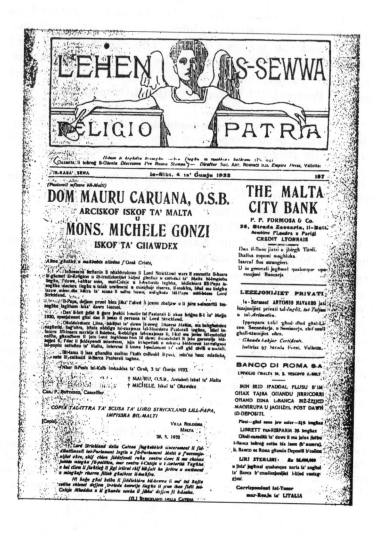

The front page of *Lehen is-Sewwa* of Saturday, 4 June. 1932 showing the Pastoral Letter of Archbishop Dom Mauro Caruana and Bishop Michael Gonzi, in which they withdrew their previous Pastoral Letter of 1 May, 1930

infiltration. Young Maltese were enrolled in the *Balilla* and *Avanguardisti*.[78]

It was in this situation that the British authorities promulgated the Seditious Propaganda Ordinance, which empowered the Governor to intercept seditious material[79] and to combat fascist and pro-Italian propaganda which was flooding the islands.[80]

Three years back, the governor had already promulgated an act called the Press Law 1929 by which the Imperial Authorities began to check the flow of propaganda from abroad. *The Prevention of Seditious Propaganda Ordinance 1932* (published in June) was the logical development of the 1929 act and it shows the preoccupation of the Imperial Authorities with the political situation in Malta. The implications of this ordinance were clearly explained in the press.[81]

By this time, the Socialist League had begun to limit its activities and lose its membership because of the attacks that never ceased during its six years of existence. However, a handful of socialist activists remained in the organization and kept the League alive, even if under adverse conditions with the Nationalists in power. In fact, on 18 September 1932, the remaining socialists met and decided on a general meeting for all members to be held on the 26th instant. During this meeting some changes in the statute of the League were discussed and Duminku Degiorgio was elected President.[82] This was to be the Socialist League's last meeting.

---

[78] Swinton, 89.
[79] *Malta Government Gazette* Supplement LXXXI, 15 September 1932.
[80] *Ibid.*
[81] E. Mizzi became Minister of Public instruction and under his administration the re-instatement of the Italian language provoked reaction from the Constitutional Party and the Labour Party.
[82] S.T. 718-719.

The Raids

The Prevention of Seditious Propaganda Ordinance was applied against the Socialist League's most prominent activists. In fact, their correspondence and activities had been attentively scrutinized by the Defence Security Office and, on 18 March 1933, the Governor, acting on information provided by the Defence Security Officer, issued warrants to the police to raid the houses of certain known leftists.[83] The houses and offices of Carmelo Carabott, Ġanni Valvo, Salvu Pulis, Ġużè Orlando, Wiġi Azzopardi, Joseph Storace, Francesco Pulis, Juann Mamo, and Ġino Muscat Azzopardi were raided at the same time.

The main reason put forward by the Governor for the raids was the desire to unearth a communist organization which had its headquarters in the Dockyard, 'which we know existed, but of which we had little actionable evidence'.[84] The British authorities also feared that this organization would grow into a movement which could have developed to menacing proportions intolerable for the security of the island fortress.[85] The Seditious Propaganda Ordinance was the instrument chosen to unearth the Socialist League and destroy its influence, especially in the most delicate area of the Dockyard, where the League had its roots and greatest following. In fact the same Governor had made an important speech to the island's parish priests during the traditional Candlemas ceremony, in February. In his speech, the Governor had asked the parish priests to use their power to help the authorities to destroy the influence of communist propoganda. The Governor also asked for all

---

[83] 'With reference to my despatch no.60 of to-day's date, I have the honour to state that acting on information in the possession of the Defence Security Officer on the subject of communistic activities in Malta, I issued warrants on the 18 th March for searching the houses of nine persons. The papers and correspondence seized are now being examined.' PAV. Des. no.60, Encl.11, Gov. D. Campbell to S.S.C., P. Cuncliffe Lister, 3 April 1933.
[84] *Ibid.*
[85] *Ibid.*

assistance necessary so that communism in Malta would be nipped in the bud.[86]

The colonial government and the local Church, which carried the ideological banner of the ruling classes, united in their efforts to destroy the very first signs of proletarian organization. The seditious material found in the possession of six out of the nine people who had their homes and properties searched 'justified the carrying out of the raids and proved that a definite subversive organization does exist'.[87] The trial which followed was an important one, especially when considered in the context of the political situation in Malta. The British authorities had unearthed and destroyed an organization for security reasons. On the other hand for the Nationalists and the Church all this was the culmination of their triumph over the reformist movement and the destruction of a revolutionary potential which had created so much alarm in their quarters. The Sedition Trial which followed was the symbolic act that destroyed the most advanced and socialistically-oriented faction of the reformist movement.

The Sedition Trial

April 28, 1933 marked the beginning of the 'Trial of the Reds', as it became known. It was to be the longest trial ever held in the Maltese law courts.[88] During all the sittings, the court hall was always full of people, many of them sympathizers of the accused.[89] The accused were Carmelo Carabott, Ġanni Valvo, Ġużè Orlando, Wiġi Azzopardi, Salvu Pulis, and Joseph Storace,

[86] 'At the same time however, knowing well the great influence that you have amongst all, the great interest which you take in their welfare, I ask your assistance in nipping in the bud that sinister communist propoganda which strikes at the very roots not only of the Church but also of all ordered society and which is seeking to insinuate itself in Malta.' 'The Candlemass Ceremony', *The Malta Chronicle and Imperial Services Gazette*, 4 February 1933.
[87] PAV., Des., no.60, Encl.11, Gov. D. Campbell to S.S.C. P. Cuncliffe Lister 3 April 1933.
[88] 'Sedition Trial in Malta', the *Times*, 14 August 1933.
[89] C. Carabott interviewed by the author.

A political caricature by A. Gerada from *Il-Berqa* of 18 March 1933 - a few days after the Sedition raids. According to this paper and to others supporting the Compact, the raids which were aimed to unearth communism in Malta were a mere blow-up.

who were charged with importing, publishing, distributing, selling, and possessing seditious matter.[90] The trial was held in Maltese and recorded in Italian. It received an enormous day-to-day coverage in most local papers and also in foreign periodicals, reviews, and daily papers. The prosecution was led by Dr German. Five of the accused were defended by Sir Augustus Bartolo while Dr Ġużè Borg Olivier defended Storace.[91]

Carmelo Carabott was accused of clandestinely circulating and selling communist, socialist, rationalist, and atheistic literature, and of trying to undermine the religious beliefs of the people in order to guide them into atheism.[92] He had been found in possession of correspondence with the Rationalist Press Association,[93] and of letters sent to him by *Carcaris* (Father Ġużepp Maurin) which expressed atheistic and anti-clerical views as well as other literature containing explicit communist propaganda.[94] More correspondence found in Carabott's

[90] S.T. 18.
[91] At first the accused chose three lawyers for their defence; Dr Magri, Dr Harding, and Dr Camilleri, who decided not to defend them at the beginning of the trial on the language pretext. The three of them were prominent pro-Italians.
[92] S. T., 191
[93] *Ibid.* 187
[94] In this Trial it became known that the writer who, used *Carcaris* and other pseudonyms was a priest by the name of Dun G. Maurin. The latter had been a Catholic cleric, but after sojourning in England became a Protestant. He had been denounced by Bishop G. Pace in a Pastoral Letter, dated 15 April 1913. (C. Sant, 'Protestant Maltese Bible Translation; The Gospel of St Mark", *Journal of Maltese Studies,* p.90)
G. Maurin was later condemned a *divinis* and left without ecclesiastical powers in a church institute. From here, he wrote various atheist and communist literature considered 'blaphemous' by the Court, and sent then by post to various prominent Leftists. Dun Maurin also had contacts and relations with members of the Socialist League, and met some of its known members frequently. The letters in which he declared himself to be an atheist and communist were read in the trial as proof of Carabott's seditious activities.
S. T., 250
After the Sedition Trial, Maurin was put on trial for contravention of the Post Act of 1924. He went through accusations of blasphemy and madness by the prosecution. His defendant stated that there was no basis to treat Maurin as such and to put him through psychiatric examinations. However, the Court decided to the contrary and Maurin was put under psychiatric observation in a lunatic Asylum (*Il Poplu,* 29 August 1933).

possession in the raids and which was declared to be seditious included letters to and from *Kniga,* Workers' Bookshop Ltd., *Concentrazione di Azione Anti-Fascista, Partito Socialista Italiano* (Paris), *Casa Editrice Repubblica* (Paris), *Liberissima* and the I.C.W.P.A.[95] Carabott had been the librarian of the Socialist League and ran a bookshop in which he sold the League's publications. He also imported socialist and revolutionary literature. Carabott had also published his Żejtun address on some of the publications of the League.[96] He had been active in the League since 1927 and had been involved in all major activities of the organization, especially in the importing, distribution, and selling of literature, even after the promulgation of the 1932 Ordinance.[97]

Ġużè Orlando was not actually a member but he was a great sympathizer and friend of the most prominent members of the League. Orlando had been the secretary of the Labour Party and one of the exponents of the left in the movement. He was accused of possessing seditious literature and correspondence with various agencies and organizations abroad, including, for example, O. Morgari the editor of the socialist paper *Avanti!.*[98] During the trial it became known that he had also been made honorary member of the Socialist Party of Italy for the help he had given to that party. Orlando was also accused of importing and distributing seditious matter.[99] He was found in possession of books considered highly seditious, such as *Lo Stato Operaio.* Furthermore, he was accused of holding in his possession machinery pertaining to the printing press which had been used by the League.[100] Ġużè Orlando was also charged with propagating class hatred both as speaker in political meetings

---

[95] S. T. 148
[96] Anon., *X'Inhu s-Socialismu?*
[97] S. T. 146.
[98] *Ibid.* 325.
[99] *Ibid.* 329.
[100] *Ibid.* 283.

and as editor of the Labour Party paper *Il Cotra*, where he had written and edited articles which were considered seditious.[101]

The charges brought against Carmelo Carabott were also brought against Ġanni Valvo, one of the main activists of the *Ghakda Socialista Maltija*. He was found in possession of seditious literature, such as *Lest We Forget* and *Daily Worker*. One of the main accusations against Valvo was that he had copies of *Il Bandiera tal Maltin*, which had been Manwel Dimech's paper.[102]

Salvu Pulis was charged with being one of the most prominent members and propagandists of the Socialist League, and that he had written pamphlets in Maltese, which had been published by the same society. His contributions included *L'Euuel ta Mejju* (1929), and *Il Faxxismu* (1929).[103] He was also accused of having in his possession the translation of the anthem, *L'Internazionale*,[104] which was considered subversive and seditious – together with various communist publications such as *L'Humanité!*, *Almanach d'Ouvrier et Paysans*, *Sempre*, *Almanacco di Guerra di Classe*, and the *Daily Worker*, the organ of the British Communist Party.[105]

Wiġi Azzopardi was one of the most revolutionary intellectuals in the Socialist League. He was accused of possessing seditious material such as the booklets *Communist Work in the Factories*[106] and *150,000,000 Starving*.[107] Azzopardi was one of the most active members and had also been elected President

---

[101] 'Che l'attivita di Orlando nello indirizzare il "Partito del Lavoro" verso i principii rossi, nonche la sua connessione coll'Ghakda Socialista risulta nei documenti esebiti in questa causa e da altre prove.' *Ibid.* 279.

G. Orlando was also charged of being in correspondence with the Vice-General Secretary of the *Concentrazione Anti-Fascista*, in Paris, even after the promulgation of the XIX Ordinance of 1932. *Ibid.* 280.

[102] *Ibid.* 260.

[103] *Ibid.* 403.

[104] *Ibid.* 406.

[105] *Ibid.* 10.

[106] *Ibid.* 371.

[107] *Ibid.* 375.

Another caricature taken from Il-Felu of April 1933.

of the League.[108] He was also editor of *Il Kuddiem! Lehen il-Haddiem Imcasbar*, a socialist periodical.[109] Seditious articles in various papers showed that Azzopardi had declared that he was a revolutionary and that he had propagated revolutionary socialist ideals.[110] The documents found at Azzopardi's private residence were, for the prosecution, clear proof that the Socialist League wanted to reach its ideals by means of revolution.[111] Many articles by Wiġi Azzopardi were considered by the court to be highly inflammatory. In writings such as *Il Haddiem u il Cleru*, Azzopardi had threatened to harm Catholic priests should they not distribute the treasures of the Church to the poor.[112]

Joseph Storace was the last to be examined by the prosecution. Storace's case was different: he had never been a member of the League, nor was he one of their intimate friends and sympathizers – as the prosecution had termed Ġużè Orlando.[113] He was accused of possessing literature which was considered incriminating[114], and of having corresponded with 'the USSR Society for Cultural Relations with Foreign Countries' and of trying to become a Soviet propagandist in Malta.[115]

In the sentence delivered by Magistrate Wirth, the Socialist League was found guilty of various crimes, the primary one being that it wanted to make Malta an international socialist republic. It was also found guilty of accepting extremist literature and of having printed and published socialist pamphlets in Maltese. The fact that the League's emblem was the hammer and sickle further increased its seditiousness.[116]

---

[108] *Ibid.* 376.
[109] *Ibid.* 364.
[110] *Ibid.* 369.
[111] *Ibid.* 364.
[112] *Ibid.* 370.
[113] 'Invero, finora non risulta che egli abbia esplicato alcuna attività pubblica o clandestina, di propoganda sediziosa.' *Ibid.*, 414.
[114] *Ibid.*
[115] *Ibid.* 415.
[116] *Ibid.* 720.

Further incriminating evidence brought against the members of the League was the fact that on 8 September – then Malta's National Day[117] – they had placed at the foot of the Great Siege Monument a wreath which carried the symbol of the hammer and sickle.

The League's contacts and association with such international organizations as the ICWPA and the Dimechian literature discovered in the residences of some of its members were all judged seditious.[118] Accordingly, the examination of these and other documents found in the possession of the accused, helped to further incriminate the Socialist League as a common criminal organization 'which made crimes against the security of the government and against public tranquillity.'[119]

The trial took thirty-five sittings. In the end Carmelo Carabott was sentenced to three months imprisonment and a £15 fine; Ġanni Valvo, to one month imprisonment and a £10 fine; Wiġi Azzopardi and Ġużè Orlando to two months imprisonment and a £10 fine each; while Salvu Pulis was fined £15. Joseph Storace was acquitted.[120] The judgements in this trial are worth pondering over. Storace was acquitted even though he had been found in possession of what was considered seditious literature, while those who were prominent activists of the Socialist League, and Orlando who was an active sympathizer of the GhSM and a known leftist, were all found guilty. This shows the political nature of the trial and that its real objective was to destroy the League. The court's decisions were appealed against. However, owing to technicalities, these appeals were rejected.[121] Eventually the Governor remitted the sentences and they were all set free.

The Socialist League was destroyed once and for all as a result of the trial, which was only overtly concerned with possession of seditious literature. The latent and most important objective

---

[117] *Ibid.* 123.
[118] The League's propaganda was considered by the prosecutor as '*intesa a promuovere malcontento e disaffezione tra i sudditi di S. Maesta.' Ibid.*, 245.
[119] *Ibid.* 232.
[120] *Ibid.* verdict by Judge L. Wirth, 14 August 1933.
[121] *Ibid.* 769.

was definitely political: the destruction of the *Ghakda Socialista*. And this objective was reached, as the Governor himself stated:

I think that the action taken by the police has had the effect of breaking up the activities of the *Ghakda* which now no longer exists, while the judgement has had the effect of serving a lesson to others who might be inclined in the same way as the accused... the trial has served a useful purpose in that it enabled undoubted communists by conviction to be eliminated from the dockyard and was thus fully undertaken.[122]

The *Daily Worker*, the British communist organ, commented on this trial giving other reasons why this was a political trial intended to eliminate the Socialist League:

Malta is the Naval fortress of Britain in the Mediterranean, and part of the war preparations that are now being pushed rapidly ahead is to terrorize the working-class of Malta, and to keep it in chains.[123]

In destroying the Socialist League, the British authorities had found the willing co-operation of the Catholic Church and the Nationalist government. With the Nationalists in government; with a weak opposition (the Labour Party had returned only Dr Paul Boffa to the legislative assembly); a destroyed reformist movement; and a defunct Socialist League; the traditional privileged classes did not fear organized local attacks on their interests anymore. Keeping by the rules and spirit of the 1921 constitutional compromise would have assured the traditional bourgeoisie hegemony over the people and governmental power. During the first days of the Nationalist government, ministers were clearly given to understand that the new constitution must be faithfully observed.[124] However, in a regional context where

[122] Gov. to Schuckburgh, 5 January 1934, quoted in Borg, 224.
[123] 'What is crime in British Malta', *The Daily Worker*, 15 August 1933.
[124] Swinton, 90.

Mussolini was renewing irredentist ambitions on Malta and other Mediterranean lands,[125] the local pro-Italian privileged classes in power had become a threat to Malta as an important unit in the British empire. Fascist activities became a familiar scene on the island, while a massive propaganda campaign was organized by the Foreign Affairs Ministry of Fascist Italy.[126] The activities of the Nationalist government became so pro-Italian, and the Fascist irredentist tendencies so pronounced, that the colonial authorities feared that their own power would be undermined and that Malta's security within the empire would be hampered. Viscount Swinton later stated that, in spite of the clear instructions which the British had given to the Nationalist government that the constitution must be observed, the latter had deliberately frustrated the language provision and attempted to undermine both English and Maltese, having sent elementary school teachers to be trained in Italy 'although the law provided that Italian should not be taught in the elementary schools'.[127]

The colonial authorities accused the Nationalist government of breaking the 1921 constitutional compromise by undermining such provisions as the language question. The government was also accused of breaking the basis on which the diarchy had been based, that is, the guaranteeing of British security on the islands in the imperial framework. The situation became so alarming for the colonial authorities that:

'Ministers were warned that all this must stop, if they were to remain in office. They refused to mend their ways. We had given them perhaps too much rope, but we wanted to give the Constitution every chance. However that may be, they certainly hanged themselves.
In November 1933 I (Viscount Swinton) instructed the Governor to dismiss the Ministers and reassume the administration of the island'.[128]

[125] A. Cassels, *Mussolini's early Diplomacy*, 86.
[126] G. Carocci, *La politica Estera dell'Italia Fascista (1925-28)*,
[127] Swinton, 90.
[128] *Ibid.*

MALTA MINISTERS DISMISSED

EVENING STANDARD

LATE SPECIAL

The poster of a late special edition of the *Evening Standard* issued on the same day the Maltese Nationalist ministers were dismissed.

The Constitution was suspended on the argument that the Nationalist Party had disregarded the conditions under which representative government had been restored and because the finances of the islands were being badly run. The 1921 compromise had come to an end and the diarchical system destroyed. Rule by direct Crown Colony government had replaced it, leaving the local traditional middle-classes with no governmental power.

6

Conclusion

The first two decades of the twentieth century were characterized by heavy unemployment in Malta. The much-needed investment in infrastructure and large enterprises did not materialize. Malta was a fortress colony, and its economy fluctuated according to the needs of the fortress which was just a cog (albeit an important one) in the machinery of the British empire.

The socio-economic condition of the Maltese working-class was thus highly critical especially after the First World War. This was one of the main causes of the June 1919 riots.

The 1921 Constitutional compromise which had produced a diarchy had secured the interests of the colonial authorities and of the traditional middle-classes but it did not minimally cater for the lower classes. So the lower classes, unlike the bourgeoisie and the Catholic Church, were directly hit by these economic fluctuations which, at their worst, left them in misery and starving. The need for industrialization was felt by the working class intellectuals and a new sector of the middle class of pro-British extraction. Industrialization was the one basic issue on which the 1926 Compact formula between the Constitutional and the Labour parties was reached. However prior to the Compact the Labour Party had sought to form a coalition with the Panzavecchians (PPM) – a coalition which was unsuccessful but which manifested the pro-clerical ideology of the Labour Party at the time.

From the mid-1920s till the early thirties, the political alignments in Maltese politics became much more complex, particularly as Fascism extended its influence in the Mediterranean. Inevitably a politico-religious dispute broke out. It was the manifestation of a struggle between two main class alliances. On the one hand was the alliance of the workers with a section of the 'modern middle-class' in the Compact reformist movement. On the other hand the alliance of the traditional clerico-landowning-professional middle-class which fused into an enormous reactionary bulwark against any reforms which would have touched the interests of the privileged classes. The Catholic Church was placed at the front of this strife so that this economic and social struggle took the semblance of a Church-State dispute at its height. This struggle left little room for political manoeuvering for the Compact parties, which had been elected to government in the 1927 elections, and had only managed to pass some rudimentary social legislation.

At the time of the 1921 Constitutional compromise, news had reached Malta of Manwel Dimech's death. He had been exiled for security reasons by the colonial authorities with the aid of the local bourgeoisie and the Catholic Church. By 1933, these forces had again fused together and triumphed over the Compact alliance between the working classes and the new progressive section of the middle classes. They then proceeded to aid the British authorities in destroying the Socialist League, the most socialistically-inclined unit in the Labour movement and which had arisen with the signing of the Compact in 1926. It was a most ideologically coherent and seriously organized proletarian association on the left of the Labour movement. In its seven years of activity, it succeeded to create a steady system of propaganda distribution–importing and circulating leftist literature as well as printing and publishing the first booklets on socialism in Maltese. The League's main activities were among the proletariat of the Dockyard. However it exerted influence in the Compact movement, the Labour leadership, and on the wider political situation.

The League's activities must also be seen in a regional and international context. The spreading of fascism, the complicated transformation and developments of the Italian left and the Italian anti-fascist movement in exile (the *GħSM* had direct and continuous correspondence with the latter in Paris), the development of British socialism after the 1926 general strike, and the diverse political struggles in the international workers' movement, all influenced the League and the Leftist elements orbiting it. The Russian Revolution was also still fresh in the minds of many Europeans and it had come to represent a focus of allegiance for the international workers' movement, including Maltese socialists.

After the 1933 raids and the sedition trial which followed and which definitely disbanded the Socialist League, most of the accused in the sedition case lost their jobs and experienced a long period of economic and social frustration. The sedition trial was the last political 'legal' act aimed at destroying the most socialistically-inclined section of the workers' movement. However, the reactionary pro-fascist orientation of the dominant classes in government led them into trouble with the other part of the diarchy: the colonial authorities. This was the result which the governing Nationalist Party (a political fusion of all the various tendencies of the traditional upper classes) brought on itself with its pro-Italian policies in a situation where Mussolini was referring to the Mediterranean as *Mare Nostrum*. The British felt that the policies of the new Nationalist government hampered the security of the island's strategic position in the British empire and suspended the 1921 Constitution. Direct rule was assumed by the colonial authorities.

It was only six years later, in 1939, that the MacDonald Constitution set up a twenty-member Council of Government (consisting of 10 elected, 2 nominated, 5 *ex-officio* members, and 3 other officials). However this constitution did not give an adequate representation. It was in fact a return to direct Crown Colony government. The 1921 Constitutional compromise had clearly failed. This state of affairs remained until the turmoils created by the Second World War, which brought definite and profound social changes in the lives of the Maltese people, climaxing with the granting of the MacMichael Constitution in 1947 – a constitution that brought a different Labour Party to power.

Plate 1

Manuel Dimech (1860-1921) : a revered hero of the working
classes; a self-made man, an intellectual and rebel who founded
Ix-Xirca tal-Imdaulin (League of the Enlightened). Having
made himself the enemy of the colonial authorities, the church
and the local privileged classes, Dimech was exiled to Egypt
where he died.

Plate 2

The cover of the novel *Ulied in-Nanna Venut fl-Amerca* (1930) written by the Dimechian Juann Mamo. In this satirical work the author gives a clinical description of the members of the *Ghakda Socialista*.

Plate 3

ITTRA ENCICLICA

TÁL

PAPA LJUN IT-XIII

"RERUM NOVARUM"

tal 15 ta Meiju, 1891,

FUK CHIF JINSABU IT-TFAL TAX-XOGHOL

MAKLUBA GHALL MALTI

MINN

P. F. BELLANTI

MAWBDEA REG-SEMBIA TAL CSISTI, MINN L'U. C. S. G.

The front page of the first translation into Maltese of Pope Leo XIII's Encyclical Letter *Rerum Novarum.*

Charles D. Plater S.J.

Plate 4

Lord Gerald Strickland - leader of the Constitutional Party and Prime Minister of the Compact government 1927-30.

Plate 5

A row at the Constitutional Party's Club in Birkirkara. Such brawls, often violent, were not uncommon.

Plate 6

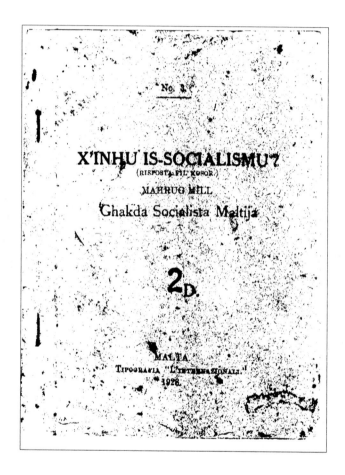

X'inhu is-Socialismu? (*Risposta fil- Kosor*) [What is Socialism? A Brief Answer] published by the Socialist League in 1928. This pamphlet was printed at *Tipografia "L'Internazionali"*, the League's own printing press.

Plate 7

Kingsway — the main street of Malta's capital city, Valletta —
always a popular site for demonstrations.

Plate 8

Mikiel Angelo Borg - one of the founders of the *Camera del Lavoro* and a prominent leftist intellectual.

Plate 9

The Grand Harbour – for decades a busy British naval base. Here, H.M.S. *Ramillies* is seen being towed off after running aground.

Plate 10

The first two pages of Uigi Azzopardi's booklet *Il-Fakar*
[Poverty] published in 1927. In a short foreword Uigi Azzopardi
strongly points out that socialism is not against religion.

Plate 11

A Labour Party public meeting held in Senglea on 19 July 1931.

Plate 12

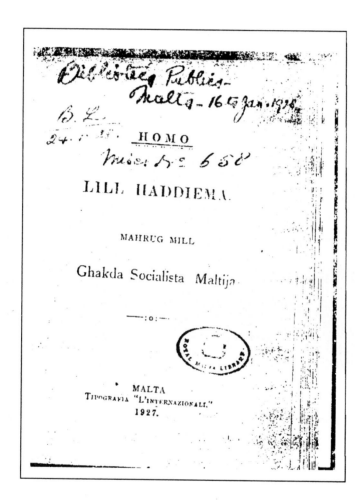

The front cover of another pamphlet published by the *Ghakda Socialista Maltia – **Lill Haddiema*** [To the Workers]. In this pamphlet released in 1927, the author, under the *nom de plume* of HOMO, gives an impressionistic exposition of the basic socialist principles.

Plate 13

Ghaqda Socialista Maltija

IL
BANDIERA HAMRA

Tal pinna oh! hutra, ucoll tal mazzp,
Gio nofs ta piazza, gio nofs ta piazza,
Bandiera 'hanra, tperper f'idejna,
Bid-dmugh i ghamejna, nfittxu 'l helsien.
Bandiera Hamra, cin il helsien,
Bandiera Hamra, f'cdan iz-zmien,
Bandiera Hamra, tad-dmugh u'a-denm,
Il haddiem talli jahcem,ghandu icollu sehem!

Haddiema hotna, oh! gens imkarrek,
Fid-dlam imgharrak, fid-dlam imgi arrak,
Cun int l'iggiarri f, Hamra Banciera,
Ii kerk ta l'g' adu, li zammna 'lsrera?
Bandiera Hamra, cin int id-driegh,
Bandiera Hamra, lill fkir mexxel:,
Bandiera Hamra, tal mahkurin,
Li bid-daul kaui tighec, mil jasai meliusin!

(cor)
Mela ninghakdu, oh! SOCIALISTI,
Demmna le natu 'l Capital sti,
Frott id-dbatija, b'ghaiakra u den mna,
Duc nubhuh ahna, ghax hu schenna::?

TIPOGRAFIA "L'INTERNAZIONALI,"
1 H 2X.

The official international anthem **The Red Flag** which was translated into Maltese (*Il Bandiera Hamra*) by Saver Delicata. It was published in this format by the Socialist League in 1928.

Plate 14

St John's Co-Cathedral (Valletta). It was here that on the morning of 8 June 1930, a number of compact supporters expressed strong disapproval towards the Archbishop for delivering the Whit Sunday sermon in Italian. This incident later became known as the Pentecoste Incident.

Plate 15

The principal ringleaders of the Pentecoste incident. Back row, standing from left to right: Charles Ritchie, Carmelo Ciantar and Constantin Micallef. Front row, sitting, from left to right: Geraldu Ebejer, Toni Darmanin, Censu Taliana and Lazzru Xuereb.

Plate 16

IL FAXXISMU (Fascism) written by Salvu Pulis, a prominent socialist intellectual. This work, which was published by the GHSM in 1929, gives a detailed exposition of the oppressive nature of Italian Fascism.

Plate 17

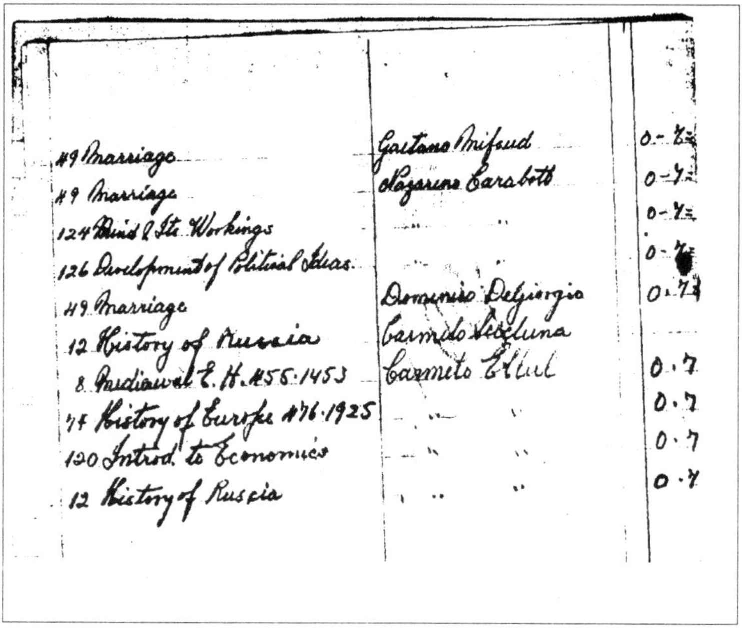

49 Marriage	Gaetano Mifsud	0-7
49 Marriage	Nazzareno Carabott	0-7
124 Mind & Its Workings	" "	0-7
126 Development of Political Ideas.	" "	0-7
49 Marriage	Domenico Degiorgio	0-7
12 History of Russia	Carmelo Scicluna	
8 Mediaeval E. H. 455-1453	Carmelo Ellul	0.7
74 History of Europe 476-1925	" "	0.7
120 Introd. to Economics	" "	0.7
12 History of Russia	" "	0.7

An extract taken from Carmelo Carabott's 1932 sales book wherein he lists not only the titles and prices of books which he sold but also the names of the people to whom he sold them. The names of Nazzareno Carabott and Duminku Degiorgio, two ardent socialists, feature in this list.

Plate 18

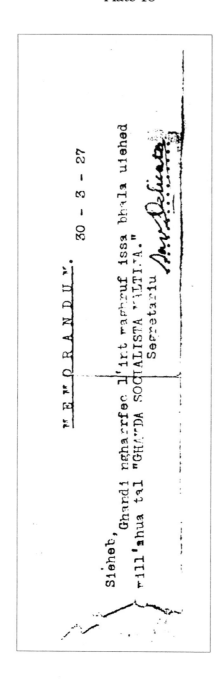

A short note sent to newly-accepted members of the Ghakda Socialista Maltia. The note reads: *"Comrade, may I inform you that you have now been accepted as a fellow of the Malta Socialist League."*

Plate 19

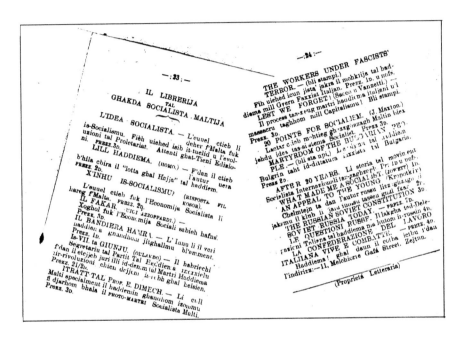

The above is a book-list featuring titles which were available for sale at the *Malta Socialist League Library*. The list, which includes both imported and locally-published literature, appears on the last two pages of the pamphlet *X'Inhu s-Socialismu?* (1928). The address of Carmelo Carabott can be found at the bottom of the book-list.

Plate 20

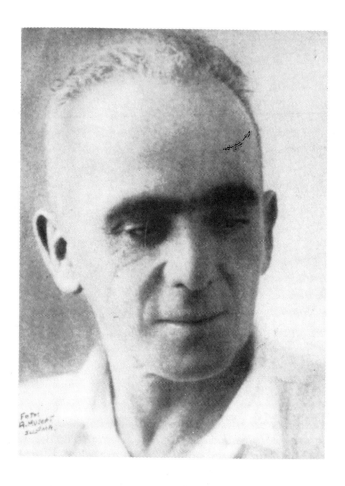

Guzè Ellul (Mercer), a socialist intellectual and writer, was, in 1928, censored by the Archbishop for his articles in *IL-HMAR*.

Plate 21

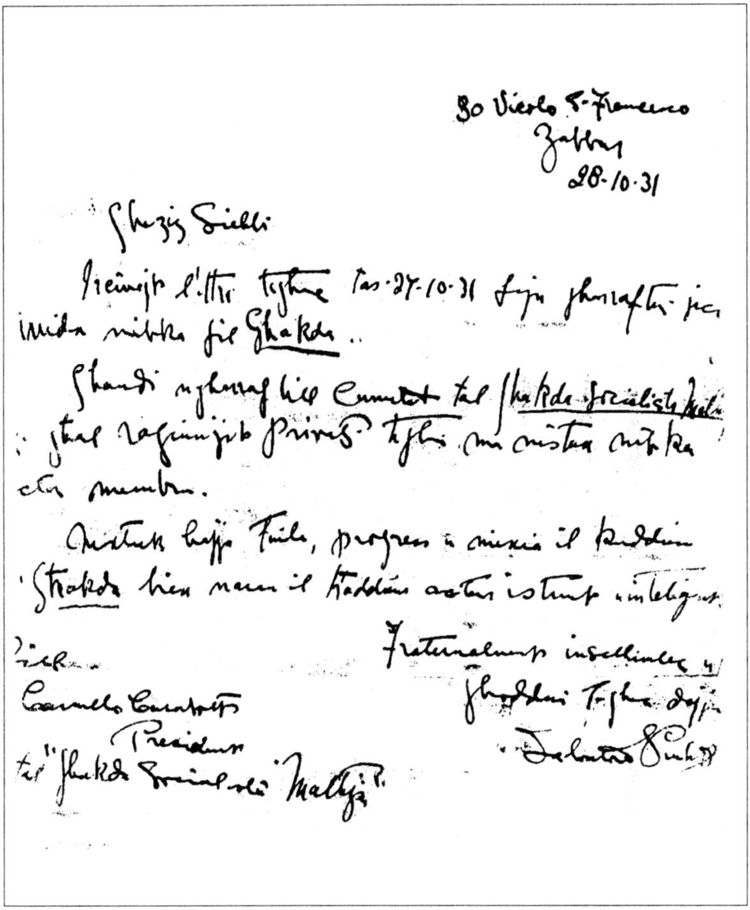

A letter sent by Salvu Pulis to the president of the Socialist League wherein the former stated that he was resigning from the *Ghakda Socialista* owing to personal reasons.

Plate 22

Maltese socialists arraigned in court for being in possession of seditious material. From left to right: Carmelo Carabott, John Valvo, Giuse Orlando, Wigi Azzopardi, Salvu Pulis and Joseph Storace.

Plate 23

Dr Paul Boffa, leader of the Labour Party, in the witness-box.

Plate 24

Joseph Borg Olivier LL.D., defence counsel for Joseph Storace.
Dr Borg Olivier was also defence counsel, alongside Professor
Sir A. Bartolo, for the other five socialists brought to court for
violating the Seditious Propaganda Ordinance.

Plate 25

On the left, Mr Gustu German, legal adviser to the Police Corps who acted as Public Prosecutor during the Sedition Trial. On the right, Mr Joseph Axisa, Second Deputy Commissioner of Police.

Plate 26

Sir Augustus Bartolo (seated) consulting with Salvu Pulis.

Plate 27

Magistrate F. Wirth LL.D. who presided over the court during the sedition case.

Plate 28

Professor Sir Augustus Bartolo Kt., LL.D., B.Litt.

Plate 29

A demonstration held by the *Partito Nazionalista* at Birkirkara in 1931.

Plate 30

Another political activity of the *Partito Nazionalista.*

Plate 31

This postcard bearing the words "The great victory of the Church and the *Partito Nazionale*" was distributed by the *Partito Nazionalista* after the 1932 general elections.

Plate 32

In *Dr Xecchec*'s view the *Partito Nazionalista* in government was serving well the clergy in Malta. Caricature extracted from *Dr Xecchec*, 26th November, 1932.

THE TRIAL OF THE REDS
The Aftermath

The **Trial of the Reds** had the immediate effect of terrorizing the working class, disorganizing its political structure and destroying its ideological orientation towards the left. The main political aims of the dominant classes and the colonial authorities were reached as the main revolutionary potential in the dockyard was destroyed.

The Labour party which had already lost ground in the previous elections found itself in disarray with its leading leftist intellectuals publicly accused of being revolutionaries and atheists, and were condemned by the Church. The publication of *Il Cotra*, the leading voice of the left, was discontinued. This weekly paper had been closely associated with leading socialist intellectuals and with the Socialist League.

Dr. Paul Boffa, the only elected Labour representative, was given unlimited powers to reorganize the Labour party. He was to accomplish this by not later than January 1934 when a General Meeting was to be held. Dr. Boffa tried to reorganize the party within the acceptable limits of the dominant Church and Empire. This can be seen in the directives which he issued to all Labour party clubs in Malta and Gozo and which included a ban on the hoisting of the red flag on the roof-tops of Labour Party clubs and the houses of activists.[1] In order to eradicate all symbolism associated with the previous left[2] which had

[1] G. Bencini, "Ittra-Cirkulari lill-Cumitati Distrettwali tal-Partit Laburista", *Il Cotra*, 30/6/1933).

[2] *ibid.*

taken root in the working class, the same directives also prohibited the singing of the Red Flag Anthem in all the activities organized by the party.

In the years following the sedition trial, but prior to the second world war, many labourites took a strictly economistic stand within local trade-unionism. Joseph Orlando, for example, became active as president of the Malta Trade Union Council and also as secretary of the *Ghaqda tal-Haddiema mal-Gvern* (Government Employees Union).[3]

As the Authorities became more sensitive to political matters in the Drydocks, many socialists remained unorganized and met only on a friendly basis and unofficially.[4] The protagonists of the Sedition Trial were only granted 'free pardon' in November 1938.[5] This pardon was hailed by *The Times of Malta*. It referred to the Sedition Case as a 'political scandal' which "occured during the Campbell-Luke Administration, when the Anti-Maltese 'Nationalists' were in power". The same article quoted Dr.Carmelo Mifsud Bonnici, who had been minister of Police at the time, as saying, at a meeting in St. George's theatre at Cospicua, that he "had conducted the Sedition Case to the satisfaction of those concerned".[6]

Leftist elements remained active in local Trade Unions, some of them subtly propagating their political ideals on paper or by word of mouth. Others were later to play a prominent role in organizing the worker's movement during the reconstruction period, after the war. However the left was never to dominate the Labour movement as it had done before the Sedition years.

---

[3] J.Orlando Smith, "Ghaqda tal Haddiema mal Gvern", *Times of Malta*, 31/12/1938.

[4] Interview of the author with C.Carabott.

[5] 'Free Pardon for all Accused in Sedition Case'. *Times of Malta*, 26/11/1938.

[6] *ibid.*

TABLES

TABLE 1

Labour Party Executive Number	1	2	3	4	5	6	7	8	9	10	11	12	13	14	15	16
Dates	1921	1922	1923	1923	1924	1925	1925	1926	1927	1928	1929	1930	1930	1931	1932	1933
Members																
Abdilla Gianni																
Aglus Carmelo							FS	FS	FS	FS		M				
Alessandro Alessandro																M
Attard Bezzina Guze														M	AT	M
Azzopardi Wigi											M					M
Bella Alfred													M	M		
Bencini Ganni	S	S	S	S	S					AS	S	S	S	S	S	S/D
Bencini Robert	M	M														
Botta Pawlu (MD)													P	P	P	P
Borg Alfons Maria	T	T	T													
Borg Guze							M	M	M	M	FS	FS				
Borg [Grech] Pawlu						VP	P									
Borg Michel	M															
Borg Mikielang									VP					VP	VP	
Bonello Gejtan				M												
Bonnici Guze (MD)									T	T	T					
Bugeja Etelvoldo		M	M		M					M						M
Bugelli Peter		M	M													
Cachia [Garreti] Ganni												M				
Caffari J.B.																
Calleja Guze	M	M	M		M	M	M	M	M	M	M		M	M		M
Carabott Nazzareno								M	M	M	M	AS	M	M	M	M
Caruana Mikiel							M	M	AD	M	M	M	M			
Casaletto Michel								M				AD	M			
Cassar Carmel (MD)												M				
Cassar Giuseppe M.												AD				
Casolani Michel (L)			M		M		M	M	M	M	M	M	M			
Cauchi Vincenzo							M	M	M	M	M	M	M		M	
Chircop Lorenzo							M						M			
Craig J.	M															
Cutajar Guze (L)	M	M					M	M	M	M	M		M	M		M
Darmanin Leone															T	M
Delia Emmanuele												M		M	M	
Demajo Pawlu	M															
Diacono Carmelo (Rev.)			M	M	M											
Ellul Guze (MD)				M	M										M	
Ellul [Mercer] Guze						M				AD	AD	D	D			M
Farrugia Vincenzo							M	M	M	M	M	VP	M	M		
Fenech Ruggiero							M									
Flores Guze																
Frendo Henry (L)		M					M	M	M	M	M		M		M	
Frenco [Azzopardi] James	M	M	AS	AS			M								T	M
Frendo Pier G. (L)	M			M	M								M	M	M	
Galea Alfred	M											M				
Galea [Balzan] Egidio (Rev.)				M			M	M	M	M	M	M	M	M		M
Gambin Edgar						M	M	M								
Gatt Gianni		M														
Gatt Guze (Rev.)		M													M	
Gatt Mose	M	M	M	M	M	M	M	M	M	M	M	M	M	AS	AS	M

P	PRESIDENT	
VP	VICE-PRESIDENT	
S	SECRETARY	
AS	ASSISTANT SECRETARY	
T	TREASURER	
A	ASSISTANT TREASURER	
D	DIRECTOR OF *IL COTRA* , THE L.P.'S OFFICIAL ORGAN	
AD	ASSISTANT DIRECTOR OF *IL COTRA*	
M	MEMBER OF L.P. EXECUTIVE	
FS	FINANCIAL SECRETARY	

TABLE 1   113

Name	Party						Reorganisation	Compact			Anti-Compact				Split			Sedition Case
Number of Executive Members	14	15	15	15	15	15	25	23	25	25	25	24	25	25	20	20	20	20
Grech Pawlu (MD)	M									M					M			
Grech Guze Maria																		
Hamilton Joseph		VP																
Hersey George			M	M	M					P	P	M					M	M
Longo Carmnu	M														M			
Magro Pawlu	M																	
Mallia Marwet						M												
Mamo Joseph E.																		
Manduca [dei Conti] Alfredo																		
Marks John F.								M	M	M	VP	T	M	M		M	M	M
Micallef Edwin																M	M	
Mifsud Armando E. (L)		M						M	M									
Mifsud Arturo	AS	AS						M				M						
Mifsud [Ellul] Guze																		M
Mifsud Filippu							AS											
Muscat [Azzopardi] Gino							M	M	D	O	O	M	M	M	AD	M		M
Naudi Edwin F.						M	M	M	M	M	AS	M	M	M	M	FS		
Olivieri Carmelo M.										M					T	M		FS/T
Orlando Guze																		
Pearman Lawrence	M																	M
Pellicano Anton																		
Portelli [Carbone] Alfredo (MD)				VP		M									VP	M	AD	
Pulis Mikiel			VP		M										M			
Pulis Salvu							T								T			
Sacco Enrico (MD)							M	M	M	M	M	M	M	M	M	M	M	M
Sammut Ugo				M				AS	AS	VP	P	P	M	M				
Sapiano Guze				P	P	P	M	M	M						M	M		
Sastariano Gianni																		
Savona William (L)	P	P	VP	P	P													
Scerri Gianni																		
Schembri Anton						M					M	M	M					
Schembri Carmelo																		
Sciberras Wenzu									M						M			
Sciduna Anton														M				
Seychell Anton	M				M		M								M			
St John Oliver																		
Valenzia Ercole (L)		M		M	M	M		M	M		M	M	M		M			
Vassallo Edgard																		
Zahra C. (MD)																	M	
Zammit Carmelo															AS			
Zammit Emmanuel							AS				M	M	M	M		M		M
Zammit Calleja C.												P	P		M			M
Zammit Harment Salvu																	FS	

Rev.   Member of the Clergy
MD   Medical Doctor
L   Lawyer/Public Notary/Legal Procurator

     Leading Leftist Intellectual

Sources: *Il Cotra*, 1928–1933.
     G. Bonnici, 1931.

NOTES TO TABLE 1

– Table 1. shows the members of the executive as they were officially elected by the party's annual general elections. Changes taking place in the composition of the Executive between official party elections are not noted here. To give an example, in the second 1922 Executive, M.L. Casolani took over Arturo Mifsud's place who in turn had taken the late Vincenzo Busuttil's place in the Legislative Assembly. In the same year Guzè Cutajar resigned and his place was taken by E.Camilleri on the 30th April. (Bonnici, G., 1931, p.52.)

– Beginning with the Eleventh (1929) Executive, the leading leftist intellectual Censu Bugeja, (who was living in Paris and working as editor of the *New York Herald Tribune* - European Edition) was unanimously acclaimed as Honorary President of the Labour Party. Because of his long absences from the day-to-day workings of the executive his name is not mentioned in Table 1.

– Robert Bencini, elected to the Labour Party Executive (1921 and 1922) resigned to join the Constitutional Party in 1922.

– The Thirteenth (1930) Executive included the greatest number of Leftist intellectuals. In fact these were the most intransigent against accepting the Archbishop's conditions to break with the Compact and stop the Party's orientation towards socialism. Together with the Constitutional Party the Labour Party was censured and voters were deterred from giving their vote to the Compact Parties in the (later suspended) immediate General Elections. The Thirteenth Executive was made up mostly of leftists because the anti-Compactist wing, led by Mikiel Caruana and Revd Egidio Galea Balzan, who wanted to accept the Archbishop's conditions, either left or were not elected to this Executive.

– Note that the Party Executive's definite orientation to the left began in 1925 with the election of prominent socialists to it.

TABLE 1   115

The year 1933 saw the end of the socialist orientation of the Executive and the end of a party which had lost ground in the last 1932 elections due to the Sedition Case.

– With the 1925 reorganization of the Labour Party, two important posts were created in the Executive: that of Director and Assistant Director of the Party's organ (which changed its name from *Labour Opinion* to *Il Cotra*). The post of Director was always held by leftist intellectuals (Gino Muscat Azzopardi, Guzè Ellul and Guzè Orlando). Before 1925 the post of Director (Ganni Bencini) of the *Labour Opinion* was not an official executive post.

– The legal profession and the clergy were the backbone of the anti-socialist, Catholic-populist wing in the Labour Party. As can be noted from Table 1 their grip on the party began to diminish as dockyard workers began to be take over. The 1930 anti-Compact split saw to the exit of the last anti-socialists from the Executive.

TABLE 2

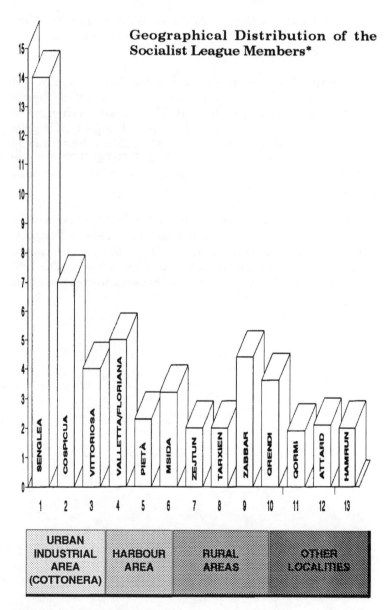

Geographical Distribution of the Socialist League Members*

*Based on the Lists exhibited in Appendix C

APPENDICES

APPENDIX A

Il-Partit Nazionali Malti

With the Compact, prominent Labour personalities made their exit from the party and together with ex-PPM activists who were against the fusion of the latter with the PDN formed the National Maltese Party (*Partit Nazionali Malti*) on 16 December 1926. Guzé Borg Pantalleresco and Dr Pier Frendo were the most prominent ex-Labourite members who worked for the creation of this new party. Dr Frendo had been a most fervent supporter of the coalition with the PPM in the 1920s. The organ of the party was *Il Patriott Malti* (later *Il Veru Patriott Malti*), and Giovanni Maria Tanti was its editor. The *Partit Nazionali Malti* (PNM) was the party of those who remained exponents of the Panzaveechian-Labour coalition ideal. However as the 'national alliance' which they tried to cement had been destroyed, these elements united to form their own party, based on the first electoral programmes of the Labour Party and the *Partito Popolare Maltese* in 1921. Logically this party took an anti-Compactist and anti-fusionist stand. Their corporatist ideology envisaged an alliance of the professional and landowning classes with the working class, and the Roman Catholic Church being the dominant hegemonic power in society. They had a communal, nationalistic conception of life, society, and politics. The *Partit Nazionali Malti* declared that their programme was based on the social encyclicals. Their manifestos stated that it was necessary for a pure Maltese nationalism to be identified and conceived from the country's history, culture, and particular necessities.

References.

Il Patriott Malti, 25 June 1927.
Il veru Patriott Malti, 2 July 1927.
Il Patriott Malti, 25 June 1927.

APPENDIX B

Draft Compact between The Constitutional Party and The Labour Party

The Labour Party and The Constitutional Party, while maintaining that the present Government does not represent the wishes of the people, even more so now that the Union Party has submitted to Dr. E. Mizzi, and now that the Government is holding on to power with the help of two members who have betrayed both their party and the electorate, these two parties, conscious of the need to take concerted action in the interest of Malta and the Maltese People, have agreed to the following:

1. That each party retain its own identity

2. That the two parties help one another and form an organized opposition to the present government.

3. That each party instruct its members in parliament to present a united front, to meet from time to time so as to cultivate an amicable relationship, provided that this agreement does not go against the Electoral Programme of either party.

4. That if the opposition is called upon to form a Ministry, should the present government resign before dissolution, the two parties shall reach an understanding, so that each party, if it so desires, shall have the right to form part of the Ministry, so that the general elections may take place.

5. That, following dissolution, each party shall help the other, and, bearing this in mind, shall recommend to the electorate that, during elections, voters shall mark their ballot paper in favour of their party's candidates and, having marked them all, shall mark also the candidates of the other party, in order of preference.

6. That, in order to prepare their supporters to vote in the manner set out in paragraph 5, each party shall, as of today, publish these instructions and recommendations in the party's

organ, and make them generally known by every possible means, such as during public meetings.

7. That The Constitutional Party, even if it should obtain an absolute majority, shall offer the Labour Party the opportunity to form part of the Ministry, in proportion to the number of deputies elected from each party; it also promises that during the first Legislature, only these measures forming part of the common programme shall be implemented, and will strive to implement the points specified in appendix "A".

8. That if any measure, not listed in Appendix "A" and appearing in the Electoral Programme of only one of the two parties, should be brought forward by the opposition for a political motive intended to defeat the government, the members of both parties shall vote against such a measure.

9. That, during the General Elections, each party shall be able to present the number of candidates specified in appendix "B".

10. That the matter of Ministerial salaries shall be discussed and decided after the present government is dissolved and before the General Elections.

Appendix "A"

1. Registration of all those who have the right to vote.

2. The amendment of the electoral law, especially where it concerns assistance to illiterate voters.

3. The Maltese Language to be the language of the courts, as is the English Language. This law comes into force after the laws have been translated into Maltese.

Proclamations and Notices to be published in Maltese as well as in English and Italian. The amendment of section 40(1) of the Constitution; that part of the section to be deleted which begins with the word 'provided' right to the end of the paragraph.

4. Fighting unemployment.

5. Assistance to be given to emigrants, with preference given to those willing to settle in the British Empire.

6. Workmen's Compensation Act.

7. Compulsory Education according to the teachings of the Church.

8. The building of schools and the renting of houses where instruction can be given.

9. Removal of customs duty on raw materials and the requirements of industry.

10. Trade Union Act.

11. Reform of the Succession Act, especially the reform of unnecessary formalities: *amendments to be effected with the consent of both parties.*

12. The encouragement of technical education.

13. Instruction in schools: as in the Labour Party's first Electoral Programme, with the addition of the following amendment: those wishing to study Italian from the junior classes may do so.

14. The building of a modern hospital for the poor.

15. The building of more houses for the workers and amending the Rent Regulation Act.

Appendix "B"

The number of candidates which each party may put forward for the General Elections.

The first District   − Labour 2 − Constitutional 3
The second District   − Labour 3 − Constitutional 3
The third District   − Labour 3 − Constitutional 3
The fourth District   − Labour 4 − Constitutional 2
The fifth District   − Labour 4 − Constitutional 2
The sixth District   − Labour 2 − Constitutional 4
The seventh District − Labour 2 − Constitutional 4
The eight District   − Labour 2 − Constitutional 4

(Source: *G. Bonnici, 1931*)

APPENDIX C

The Socialist League Membership (GHSM)

Taken from *Dichiarazioni ghad-Dhul fil-Ghakda* and another document entitled *Altra Lista di Associati all'Ghakda Socialista Maltia*, ST 1933.

	MEMBERS	ADDRESS	OCCUPATION
1	Carabott Carmelo	11, Melchiore Gafa Str., Zejtun	Dockyard
2	Valvo Ganni	28, Sda S. Angelo, Senglea	Dockyard
3	Flores Guzè	59, Sda Stretta, Valletta	Cigarette manufacturer
4	Pulis Francesco	10, Sda San Giuliano, Senglea.	Dockyard
5	Farrugia Carmelo	115, Sda Miratore, Floriana	Dockyard
6	Farrugia Wigi	171, Sda Due Porte Senglea	Dockyard
7	Vella Duminku	7, Sda Xintilli, Tarxien	
8	Chetcuti Guzè	38, Sda Tomaso Dingli, Zabbar	
9	Agius Emanuele	100, Sda Marina, Cospicua	Dockyard
10	Agius Guzè	100, Sda Marina, Cospicua	Dockyard
11	Magrin Antonio	42, Sda. Chiesa, Zabbar	
12	Ellul Guzè*	19, Sda Sofia,Cospicua	
13	Laiviera Ernesto	23, Sda Desain, Vittoriosa	Dockyard
14	Chircop Lorenzo*	73, Sda Scolastica, Vittoriosa	Dockyard
15	Zaffarese Giuse	69, Sda Vittoria, Senglea	Dockyard
16	Degiorgio Duminku	7, Sda Dolori, Senglea	Dockyard
17	Pulis Salvu*	6, Vicolo Biccieni, Zabbar	Marquis Scicluna Brewery
18	Galea Alfred *	14, Sda Michele, Senglea	
19	Gerada Michele	8, Vicolo Molo, Pietà	
20	Glanville Wigi	101, Sda Vittoria, Senglea	Dockyard
21	Chetcuti Anton		
22	Chetcuti Carmelo		
23	Galea Wigi	139, Sda Oratorio Cospicua	

24	Demosani Carmelo	c/o Lux Press, Valletta	Printer
25	Bugeja Anton	"Agent" Qormi	Agent
26	Sorreo Alfredo	134, Sda Punta, Senglea	Dockyard
27	Ciantar Carmelo	43, Sda Teatro, Valletta	Shopkeeper
28	Micallef Antonio	4, Sda Maria, Cospicua	
29	Gatt Emmanuele	26, Sda S.Angelo, Senglea	Dockyard
30	Scerri Paulu	4, Sda Crocefisso, Senglea	
31	Zerafa Nazzareno	264, Sda Due Porte, Senglea	
32	Apps Thomas	10, Spencer Monument Hill, Mile End	
33	Ritchie Charles	20 Sda Alexandria, Vittoriosa	Dockyard
34	Dougall R.	26, Sda Porta Burmola, Cospicua	
35	Borg Guzè	24, Sda L'Immacolata, Cospicua	
36	Cini Guzè		
37	Muscat G. Celestino	1, Sda Parrochiale, Qrendi	
38	Micallef Wigi	16, Sda S. Anna, Qrendi	
39	Vella Guzè	10, Sda S.Michele, Senglea	Dockyard
40	Azzopardi Wigi*	21, Sda Reale, Attard	Dockyard
41	Apap Leone	60, Molo Misida, Msida	
42	Galea Guzè	5B, School Street, Hamrun	University student
43	Schembri N.		
44	Chetcuti Clo.		Dockyard
45	Arena Guzè		
46	Delicata Guzè		Dockyard
47	Refalo Pawlu[1]	168 Sda Ponente, Senglea	
48	Mallia Wenzu		Dockyard
49	Gatt Gianni*	Senglea	Bookseller
50	Vella Censu[2]		
51	Mifsud Carmelo[3]		
52	Zarb C.[4]		

* denotes person listed as member of the L.P. Executive at some period between 1921 - 1932.

[1] ST. 138
[2] ST. 66
[3] ST. 139, and also referred to in Juann Mamo *Ulied in-Nanna Venut fl'Amerca*.
[4] *ibid.*

NOTE A Many of the above members of the GHSM, such as Duminku Degiorgio, Nestu Laiviera, Wenzu Mallia and Carmelo Ciantar were later (after 1932) to be elected Executive Committee members of the L.P. Many of the above were also members of the L.P. District Committees. These were the most important leftist intellectuals who influenced the Labour Party's orientation to the left.

NOTE B GHSM members are listed in their original order as found in *Dichiarazioni ghad dhul fil Ghakda* and another document entitled *Altra lista di Associati all'Ghakda Socialista Maltia* ST. 1933.

However, the last three names are not found in the above official documents, but are taken from other sources which are referred to. There are other names of prominent persons in the GHSM (such as Saver Delicata who was a founding member of the ghakda) which are not listed in the official documents.

A TRANSFORMING
VIEW

Programme of the United-Anglo-Maltese and Maltese Constitutional Parties. To be known henceforth as the Constitutional Party

(1) The Party will do all in its power to ensure the smooth and proper working of the Constitution, so as to secure to the people of Malta the fullest possible advantages as a self-governing nation of the British Commonwealth.

(2) The Party takes its stand on three basic principles, viz:-
   (a) steadfast observance of the Roman Catholic Religion, the religion of our forefathers.
   (b) strict preservation of Maltese national individuality.
   (c) sincere loyalty to the British Crown and close union with the British Empire; and in pursuance of these three cardinal points, will make its duty:-

   (a) To make a solemn profession of faith and "associate with the inauguration of the legislature and its future deliberations the service and the benediction of the Church of our fathers".
   (b) to live up to the great traditions of our race, inspiring the people with confidence in the future; and
   (c) to enable them to realise and reap the full benefits of their proud position as one of the communities of free nations that constitute the British Empire.

(3) The Party will abide by the provisions of the Letters Patent enacting the Malta Constitution with regard to the language question in all their aspects and bearings, and will give equal facilities for the learning of both English and Italian.

(4) So long as the Government cannot provide sufficient school accomodation to make it possible to eventually introduce Compulsory Education adequate provision shall be made to meet the requirements of those who are at present seeking, but cannot obtain, admission into the schools; subsidies are to be given to private educational institutions that relieve the Government of

part of its duties left unfilled through lack of money and building materials. Meanwhile all possible measures will be adopted to raise both the standard of education and the status of teachers.

(5) No new taxation is to be proposed, but on the contrary, retrenchment in the administration will be attempted consistent with the vested interests of all persons and of Government employees of whatever grade.

(6) All the resources of the Islands will be fully explored and exploited and the revenue carefully administered so as to avoid undue burdens. The Imperial Government will be asked to release such property as is no longer required for Imperial purposes.

(7) The Party will consider the advisability of adopting the Workmen's Compensation Act.

(8) Trade, Commerce and Agriculture will be encouraged and assisted in every possible way.

(9) Measures will be considered for strengthening existing industries, reviving such as are practically extinct, and creating new ones.

(10) The members of both Houses are to be paid £150 per annum and ministers are to have the same salary as judges and to give the whole of their time to the service of the state. They are to suspend the exercise of any other profession for their own private gain during their tenure of Office.

(11) The Civil Service and the Police are to be safeguarded from political interference, and careful attention bestowed on their interests.

(12) Government lands and houses are to be given on long lease to a fair valuation in order to encourage improvements and

productivity and to find work for labourers. Sitting tenants will have preference in competition with other applicants.

(13) The most is to be made of the resources and attractions of Malta as a tourist centre of unique interest and an exceptional field of archaeological research.

Malta Herald, Sept. 2, 1921.

D.M.C. – 14th September 1921
The Labour Party Electoral Programme – 1921

The Party enters the Political Arena for the first time in our History, equipped with the principles of Democracy, Honesty and Justice under the noble motto: "Pro Aris et Focis".

The Party solemnly declares in the inauguration of the first legislature of the new Government, to affirm the predominance of, and to defend, the Roman Catholic Religion, and to associate the prayers and benediction of the Church as the pivot of all its foundations and deliberations.

The Party undertakes to defend the interests of the Maltese People in general and, more especially so, the interests of the working classes, guided by the golden rules of Christian democracy, and to promote to the fullest possible extent the economic, moral, technical and intellectual interests of those who depend on their exertions, by hand or by brain, for the means of subsistence.

The Party, fully recognizing the great difficulties which may possibly confront its political progress, do not wish to hold out any mystical or gilded promises, with a view to obtaining support or enlisting sympathy at the elections, but, nevertheless, it binds itself honestly and faithfully, so far as it lies in its powers, to treat as most paramount the following fundamental points:-

1 – Education
Compulsory Education, under the control and guidance of the Roman Catholic Church, will be the principal and primary aim of the Party, including a higher standard of elementary and technical education and the ameliorating of the status of those entrusted with the scholastic progress of our future generations, with a view to removing once for all the stain of illiteracy which prevails amongst the majority of the population of these Islands.

Owing to the present limited school accommodation, and until such time as the Government may be able to facilitate additional accommodaton to meet the increased influx due to compulsory education, the Government will be asked to grant subsidies to the various Monasteries, Convents or other private scholastic institutions to instruct the younger generations, (where they would be willing to undertake this duty?)

II – Unemployment

This burning and serious question will be treated with the utmost vigour, and the Party will give careful attention to the promotion and encouragement of existing local and other new industries, and the revival of such industries as may have declined; it will fully exploit the agricultural resources of the Islands and will insist, so far as compatible with local conditions, on the removal of taxes on raw materials in order to give every facility and protection to local production.

III – Emigration

The Party will use its utmost endeavours to cause all restrictions on intending emigrants to be removed at once, the literacy test to be rendered efficient; and to fully encourage emigration, even by small Government grants, and possibly to obtain indulgence passages to parts of the Empire to intending emigrants.

Until such time that these questions shall be on a more salutary basis, and emigration facilitated and restored to the fullest possible extent, the liberty of alien labour is to be restricted as much as possible, and a tax be imposed on capital ammassed by foreigners on their leaving the Island.

IV – Laws

Every systematic and prudential means will be restored to raise the status of the working classes, both as regards wages, hours and conditions of employment, and will move the enaction of the following Acts:-

(a) The Workmen's Compensation Act.

(b) Old Age Pension Act.

(c) Trade Union and Factory Acts.

(d) National Insurance Acts (Emphasizing the fact that the Govt. must be the "Model Employer").

(e) The institution of a National Lottery.

(f) An Act to regulate the increase and decrease of house-rents;

(g) An Act removing restrictions on public meetings.

V – Work

The Party will by every possible means in its power endeavour to establish a small ship-repairing industry in the Island, with facilities for small construction, and to promote and encourage every facility for the execution of repairs to Merchant and other vessels by such an establishment, in order to relieve the present state of unemployment.

VI – Language

The Party, having carefully considered this delicate and important question from every point of view, has arrived at the following conclusions:-

(a) Maltese to be taught for two years in the Elementary Schools;
(b) English to be taught in the Elementary Schools up to, and including, the 4th Standard;
(c) English and Italian to be taught from the 5th Standard upwards;
(d) English and Italian to be obligatory in the Lyceum and University.

VII – Release of Imperial Property

The Party will consult the Imperial Authorities on the question of possible release of such lands and buildings which may be not required for strategic purposes, in order to increase the existing limited school accommodation, reduce the expenses due to the upkeep of present hired school buildings, and to increase the agricultural output of the Island by cultivating any such released lands.

VIII – Service under Imperial Government

The Party will urge and recommend the enrolement of able-bodied persons for voluntary service in the Forces of the Empire whether for foreign or local service, and under similar conditions and emoluments as laid down by the Imperial Authorities for corresponding units in the United Kingdom.

IX – Taxation

The Party undertakes to carefully investigate this important and unavoidable question, with the scope of adjustments where possible, although, honestly speaking, it declares its probable inability to effect any immediate reduction, it will endeavour to remove all taxes on the import of raw material in order to promote local production against similar articles of foreign produce, and by taxing manufactured imported goods at an *ad valorem* tax in such a manner that local industries and any new ones will be able to reap a profit, controlled by the State, and at the same time encourage and promote local labour, with a fair standard wage.

The party will consider the best way of gradually introducing economy in the expenditure of the local Administration, and will introduce a tax on income (Income Tax) if required by circumstances.

(sgd.) Savona

(sgd.) Bencini
Secretary.

MALTA LABOUR PARTY
ELECTORAL PROGRAMME

The Labour Party, guided by the teachings of the Catholic Church in matters of social interest, affirms the following principles:

a) Abolition of the Senate
b) Abolition of the duty on wheat
c) Introduction of the Land Tax
d) Abolition of the plurality of Votes
e) Laws necessary for the welfare of the working Classes; as the Party moreover feels the necessity of fighting the Government at present in power it will, in union with the Constitutional Party work towards this object with the view — should the two parties come into power — of putting into force, in the first Legislature, the following measures:

1. *INSTRUCTION:*
    a) Compulsory instruction in Government Schools in the Maltese language only;
    b) Education Reforms;
    c) Technical Schools.
2. *LANGUAGES:*
    a) The Maltese Language to be placed on the same footing as the Italian in the administration of the Island and on the same footing as the English Language in the Law Courts.
    b) The Maltese Language to be taught first in the Schools and the English afterwards, up to and including the 4th. Standard. Italian will be taught from the 5th. Standard and in previous standards also to those who may so desire.

3. BILLS:
   a) Workmen's Compensation Act.
   b) Trade Union Act.
   c) Amendments of the Rent Restriction Bill, the Succession
      Duty Bill and the Electoral Laws.
4. TAXATION:
   Abolition of indirect taxes on raw materials required for
   local industries.
5. BUILDINGS:
   Construction of workmen's dwellings and of a modern
   hospital.
6. OTHER MATTERS:
   a) Registration of all persons entitled to vote.
   b) Assisted passages to intending emigrants especially to
      those willing to settle in territories under the British
      Flag.
   c) Measures tending to reduce unemployment.
   d) Economy in the administration of the island.
In order that the above may be effected it will be necessary
      to build new schools or hire buildings to be used as such.
7. MINISTERS' SALARIES:
According to the Compact entered into between the Labour
and Constitutional Parties the amounts of Salaries are to be
fixed after the dissolution of the Government and before the
General Election. Such amount will be therefore inserted in our
programme in due course.

Source: Labour Opinion, 8th July, 1926.

The General Committee of the Workers' Party (1922)

We think it is most fitting that we should publish, in this issue, the names of the delegates which form the above-mentioned Committee.

I Workers' Union Br. No. 1.
      1. Joseph Hamilton - **Vice-President**
      2. Carmelo Longo

II Workers' Union Br. No. 2.
      3. Lawrence Pearman
      4. Vincenzo Portanier
      5. Paolo Mifsud

III Workers' Union Br. No. 3.
      6. Revd Gius Gatt, J.C.D.
      7. Oliver St. John

IV St. Lawrence Club, Vittoriosa
      8. Giuseppe Mallia
      9. Giuseppe Caruana
      10. Gaetano Fabri

V "Unione" Workers' Orchestral Society, Zabbar
      11. Giuseppe Tabone

VI Printers' and Compositors' Union
      12. Salvatore Dimech
      13. Carmelo M. Olivieri
      14. Paolo Buttigieg

VII "Maria Mater Gratiae" Philharmonic Society, Zabbar
      15. John Corrado
      16. Francesco Grech
      17. Emmanuele Testa

VIII "San Giuseppe" Philharmonic Society, Hamrun
    18. Giovanni Satariano

IX Dockyard Benefit Society
    19. Peter Bugelli
    20. Giuseppe Calleja

X Workers' Benefit Society
    21. Nicola Attard
    22. Aronne Galea

XI Musical Union
    23. Alberto Vella
    24. Alfredo Galea Grech

XII "G.M. De Paule" Philharmonic Society, Paola
    25. Antonio Nicholas
    26. Francesco De Giovanni
    27. Emilio Camilleri

XIII Dockyard Labourers' Benefit Society
    28. Dr. Alfonso Portelli Carbone
    29. Paul Mangion
    30. Giuseppe Gatt

XIV Imperial Government Workers Benefit Society
    31. Edgar Vassallo
    32. Giuseppe Gonzi

XV "S. Guzeppe" Mutual Help Society, Hamrun
    33. Salvatore Borg
    34. Carlo Satariano

XVI Imperial Government Workers' Union
    35. Alfonso M. Borg - **Treasurer**
    36. Giuseppe M. Grech
    37. Antonio Lubrano

XVII "St Patrick's" Workers' Club, Zabbar
    38. Dr. Antonio Cremona
    39. Giuseppe Dougall
    40. Carmelo Micallef

XVIII Goldsmiths' and Silversmiths' Association
    41. Domenico Tanti
    42. Giuseppe Matrenza
    43. Emmanuele Azzopardi

XIX "Vilhena" Philharmonic Society, Floriana
    44. Felice Debono
    45. Francesco S. Zahra

XX "Beland" Philharmonic Society, Zejtun
    46. Giuseppe Dalli

XXI Malta Dredgers' Union
    47. Giuseppe Attard
    48. George Hersey
    49. Raffaele Bugeja

XXII Central Club, Sliema
    50. E. Armando Mifsud, P.L.
    51. Gaetano Mifsud

XXIII "S. Francesco" Mutual Help Society, Zabbar
    52. Revd Carmelo Diacono
    53. Michele Cassar

XXIV Admiralty and Royal Dockyards Draughtsmen's
    Association
    54. Joseph Agius
    55. Moses Gatt
    56. Joseph Sammut

XXV "S. Francesco d'Assisi" Mutual Help Society,
     Cottonera
     57. Michele Schembri

XXVI "La Valette" Philharmonic Society, Valletta
     58. Hon. Salv. Zammit Hammet
     59. Carmelo M. Mercieca
     60. Silvio Mercieca, P.A.A.

XXVII "Prince of Wales" Philharmonic Society,
      Vittoriosa
     61. Giuseppe Schembri
     62. Salvatore Gonzi
     63. Paolo Xuereb

XXVIII Carpenters' Union
     64. Martino Vassallo
     65. Giuseppe Attard

XXIX Tram Employees
     66. Gaetano Francalanza
     67. Vincenzo Cirillo

XXX Waiters
     68. Domenico Muscat
     69. Emmanuele Cauchi

XXXI "Annunziata" Philharmonic Society, Tarxien
     70. Carmelo Mamo
     71. Carmelo Mangion
     72. Giovanni Sant

XXXII "Duke of Edinburgh" Philharmonic Society
      Vittoriosa
     73. Giorgio Peresso
     74. Lorenzo Bonanno

XXXIII Ship Repairing Shop Benefit Society, Dockyard
75. Fortunato Cauchi
76. Raffaele Solazzo
77. Emmanuele Grixti

XXXIV National Sailors' & Firemen's Union
78. Ercole Valenzia, P.L.
79. Matteo Morana
80. Antonio Spiteri

XXXV Barbers' Union
81. Not. M. Casolani - **Assistant Secretary**
82. Antonio Galea
83. Carmelo Ellul

XXXVI "Il Famiglia" Mutual Help Society, Vittoriosa
84. Giovanni Pellicano
85. Aronne Galea

XXXVII Director of Works Department Mutual Help
Society
86. Giuseppe Bonello
87. Edgar Naudi
88. Emmanuele Mercieca

XXXVIII "St. Georges" Philharmonic Society,
Cospicua.
89. Michele Grech
90. Ignazio Giusti

XXXIX Chamber of Labour and Organizers of the
General Committee
91. Hon. Col. W. Savona - **President**
92. Giovanni Bencini - **Secretary**
93. Carmelo Bonello
94. Gaetano Bonello
95. Giacinto Tua, P.L.
96. Agostino Matrenza
97. Guglielmo Arena

XL "S. Elena" Philharmonic Society, Birkirkara
    98. Alessandro Tanti
    99. Michele Borg, P.A.A.

XLI   Union of Government Minor Staff Employees
    100. Lorenzo Mallia
    101. Luigi Formosa
    102. Antonio Ferranti

XLII "S. Andrea" Philharmonic Society, Luqa
    103. Giorgio Caruana
    104. Antonio Micallef.

Labour Opinion, 29 June, 1922.

Note: The 1922 General Committee of the Labour Party, brought together delegates from the Trade Unions, Guilds and Band Clubs. Members in this committee came from all walks of life so much so that we find clerics, members of the professions (medical, legal, etc.) and ordinary workers. Note also that the organizers of this General Committee are the seven representatives from the "Camera del Lavoro" (cf. XXXIX, members nos. 91-97).

Senglea and Msida Labour Party 1932 District Committees

The following are the 1932 officially elected District Committees of two of the most militant localities: Senglea and Msida. The majority of the committee officials and members were socialist activists. It is worth noting here, the contrasting differences between the 1922 Labour Party General Committee and these two committees.

Senglea Labour Party District Committee – 1932

Honorary Presidents	Censu Bugeja, M.A.
	Dr. Pawlu Boffa
Deputy Hon. President	Carmelo Zammit
President	John F. Marks
Vice-President	Alessandro Alessandro
Secretary	Carmelo Garzia
Assistant Secretary	Guzè Azzopardi
Treasurer	Leone Darmanin
Members	Guzè Cassingena
	Guzè M. Cassar
	Francesco Cioffi
	Nicola Pace
	Carmelo Pampanella
	Guzè Urry
	Rogantine Pisani
	Guzè Caruana

(Cumitat Distrettwali ghal 1932, *Il Cotra*, 14/1/1932)

Msida Labour Party District Committee – 1932

President	Guzè Ellul
Vice-President	Guzè Orlando
Secretary	E. Micallef
Assistant Secretary	D. Apap
Treasurer	Carmelo Zammit
Members	Emmanuele Mallia
	Guzè Troisi
	Anton Stellini
	L. Troisi
	Ganni Zammit
	T. Azzopardi
	F. Spiteri
	S. Borg
	J. Pugliesevich
	E. Camilleri

(Cumitat Distrettwali Msida - 1932, *Il Cotra* 14/1/1932)

VIEWS FROM THE LEFT

FROM "L'INTERNAZIONALI" TO "THE MOON PRINTING PRESS"

The antagonistic turn which the local social contradictions took through the church-state dispute, led the Church authorities to censure the Compact and the Socialist press. At this point, the Socialist League changed the name of its printing press from "L'Internazionali" to "The Moon Printing Press".[1]

The direct anti-clerical and socialist tone of the literature printed by the Socialist League in the first two years of the thirties made the change in name imperative. As the press censorship of the Church was tightening up with numerous condemnations, the Socialist League remained the only organization with a completely free press in Malta.

One of the most eloquent writers whose 'hard-hitting' articles where printed by "The Moon Printing Press" was Censu Bugeja (also Honorary President of the Labour Party) who sent his writings to prominent members of the League from his residence in Paris. Bugeja was attacked for his association with this printing press in a vehement manner by the reactionary press.[2]

Other Compact leaders, not necessarily socialists also used this printing press to express their political stand against the local Church authorities.[3]

Carmelo Carabott who was the nominal proprietor of the printing press as well as the main printer, himself published a hand bill entitled "L'Aide Memoire",[4] where he criticized the Church authorities for their reactionary stand against the freedom of the press.[5] The distributors of "The Moon Printing

---

[1] C. Carabott in a letter to Mr. Pike of the Rationalist Press, dated 18/9/1930.S.T. p.189.

[2] "Tuegiba minn Malti lil Censu Bugeja", *Il Poplu*, 28/5/1930.

[3] C. Carabott in a letter to Mr. Pike of the Rationalist Press, dated 18/9/1930.

[4] *ibid.*

[5] *ibid.*

Press" literature where rounded up many times by the police. Some were arrested and fined. For printing the hand bill already mentioned, which according to the Courts included direct insults to the Archbishop, Carabott was fined five pounds.[6]

Two months later, in a self-advertising letter, Carabott wrote:

> ... the maltese papers refused to print fearing the Bishop's censure, I, unafraid of both censure and excommunication changed the name of the press into "The Moon Printing Press" edited the said articles, and, as might be expected my publications were censured... Perhaps most interesting of all is that I was cited by the Police and fined £5 on the 26th of July last, for having insulted the Archbishop of Gozo in a leaflet entitled "L'Aide Memoirs" distributed on 13/14th June thus violating article 10 of the Press Law of 1929 calling him "ambitious and aggressive ..." Is it not equally daring to publish leaflets calling the bishops liars and suggest the solution of the present question by the encameration of all ecclesiastical property..."[7]

---

[6] "Ahbarijiet ta Malta", *II Poplu*, 28/7/1930.

[7] C. Carabott in a letter to Mr. Pike of the Rationalist Press dated 18/9/1930.

OUR MISSION

We have nothing to lose except to give, that is to help and teach the working class which, so far, has failed to recognise its movement here in Malta. We should teach this class about the rights it has in the world, the rights it ought to have. Our mission is to publish instructive books, to show the moneyed class and the professional class that the very workers are participating to set the labour movement and the workers' movement going; those who till this very day, still seek to enslave the workers' minds, those so-called patriots, under the yoke and mantle of hypocrisy.

We have nothing to lose except to give to our brethren, since, once we have come to this world, we should help one another and defend each other as brothers would. We do not behave as some double-faced people do who, in order to obtain votes, go up to the illiterate workers and pour out a stream of meaningless words; that they are descended from this and that stock and related to that other family. They then utter one or two swear words to pass for low-class people, drink with the workers, and when they become deputies, when they are elected to parliament, God forbid that you should so much as look at them.

We do not want to become ministers, not even deputies; but we do want to see the working class educated, well-paid for their work and living in a world of bliss and peace. Our mission is very different, because what we want to do is entirely new for Malta, moreover it is also difficult because we do not have the money to do it; but above all there is the IDEA AND THE WILL which are stronger by far than "Mammon" the god of money.

This first book which we have brought out, we succeeded in publishing with money collected from subscribers to *The Maltese Proletarian Union*, and the money we take in from the sale of this book will be invested in another book we intend to publish.

Therefore we wish to see this first socialist book in Maltese purchased by the workers and read attentively by them, so that our mission may not prove futile, because the mission in which we have participated, is not a mission of deception as is that of the enemy of the workers, those enemies who have never, till this very day, shown any interest in helping the poor classes, intellectually or financially.

Workers! It is we ourselves who have to defend our rights, and we feel that we must defend them as we endure our poverty, as we endure our work, as we endure the torture of our employers, as we sweat, that sweat which pours out of us, that sweat from which there emerged the *sacred ideal* which we want to defend against the enemies of the class of misery.

Workers! Take heart! Come with us and read this book with great attention, and from it instill in your hearts the SOCIALIST IDEAL which will never leave your heart if not in DEATH.

The Maltese Proletarian League

"WE EXPLAIN"

In these days all the countries of the world have many political parties. Every party has faith in some programme or political system, with which it considers the country could go ahead of the others. But the two most popular systems are Socialism and Capitalism.

What is Capitalism?

Capitalism is that political system by which most governments throughout the world are guided; that system which admits private property, namely that an individual might possess £30,000,000 and more in a world having 2,000,000,000 people and a capital of £2,000,000,000 and that in consequence it is impossible for everyone to have his portion except in a world having only 70 persons. Therefore Capitalism is that system which allows the individual to possess as much as he likes without interference from the Government.

What is Socialism?

Socialism is that system which we would like to see supreme; that system which requires property to be public, that is belonging to everybody and not to a few, as it is today; that system which requires all wealth throughout the world to be everybody's.

And how can this wealth be everybody's?

The father and representative of all is the government or those few people whom we choose to govern us. Therefore what belongs to the government, belongs to everybody. If then the mills belonged to the government, and the imported wheat were brought here by the government, these would have belonged to the people and the profits derived therefrom would have gone to the public coffers. The government owns the water, the electricity and the post, and should likewise own land, buildings, banks, industries etc. In this way the people would be depending on themselves and not on a few persons whose interest is only that of sucking the people to their best ability. In order to bring 'this about Socialism wants, above all, that land, buildings, banks and big industries should belong to the Government, that commercial relations with other countries should be under government control; a tax on rents that increases proportionately with such rents, compulsory education, that workmen should not work more than 44 hours in a week, that wages be fixed by Trade Unions, that these Unions fix a Minimum Wage, government financial support for the unemployed and of those unable to work, equal rights for all.

These are the principal things which Socialism wants and this is what we mean by saying we are Socialists.

MALTESE SOCIALIST UNION

Extracted from The Mid-Day Views, 3rd November 1931, p.3.

THE TWO POWERS

That the evolution of a people is brought about by means of instruction is an undeniable truth.

That here in Malta we are not evolved can be clearly seen, as also the fact that the Maltese people lack that instruction which permits them to think for themselves without the need to resort to their betters, who are their betters simply because they can read and write, for every triviality.

Malta is divided into two classes: those who can write, the educated class, and those who are unable to read, the illiterate class.

The difference creates classes in every nation. It is only natural that the illiterate person approaches a member of the educated class shyly and with bowed head. So also the educated person gives himself airs as he stands before that poor illiterate man.

From this situation of the people forming a nation are born those classes which we call dominating and dominated.

It is all too natural that those who feel superior to others expect that they should rule over those who are beneath them. It is likewise natural that those in power should do their utmost in order not to lose their power.

This is exactly what the dominating class is doing in Malta: through dearth of instruction this class is holding on to power in the country, and is doing all it can in order not to lose this hold.

How? By seeking to deprive the people of instruction, and thus keep them underfoot and subjugated, whatever happens.

Because of this ignorance the learned class teaches the people to suffer patiently through all that befalls them. Because of this ignorance it teaches the people to work for fourteen hours for little pay. Because of ignorance the learned class teaches the illiterate people to keep back and not involve themselves in matters where they have a sacred right to involve themselves.

Woe betide that person who is not mean! Woe betide the man whose heart beats hard at the sight of the dominated classes! Woe betide the man who would wish to destroy the chains around the necks of the illiterate people!

The man who rebels against so much baseness will be called a madman and locked up in a lunatic asylum.

This man will be called a revolutionary and accused of wanting to change "the present state of things": the self-same "state of things" brought about by men because they were strong.

The learned class is uniting, and there is now nothing else to be done except for the illiterate class to unite likewise, so that when these two forces meet, they will not fight that one of them may be destroyed; rather both will be destroyed, that by their death one class may be born — the Class of Justice.

Gino Muscat Azzopardi

BOLSHEVISM

Bolshevism means masses. Bolshevism means government by the masses for the good of the masses. It is Communism... Where is this Bolshevism, or Communism, to be found? It is to be found only in Russia. But what forced the masses to want to govern on their own behalf for their own good and not to remain as they were in the past, ruled by the few? The reason was that the Russian masses had been too severely oppressed by their own government of the few, just as our government is oppressing the Maltese people.

We will not go into the merits of whether the Russian people are better off now than they were in the past; it is certain that the "few" are worse off, to be sure. All we want to say is that what happened in Russia can happen all over the world, even in Malta. And there is nothing, nothing is affording better propaganda for "communism" than the oppressive actions of the government. We do not speak out because we are faced with the seditious propaganda act, but we know, because we have read world movements, and we have found, and are now seeing that in Malta we have set off on the road of oppression which has caused other countries to come to an appointment with freedom. We know, and well do we know, the insults (levelled at the masses), even though little importance is being attached to them today. Yet this insult campaign if kept up, day in, day out, may lead to an explosive situation.

We do forgive, but we will never forget. As workers we do feel the insults which we forgive, however we report them to others and do not forget them. We still smart under the insult of those who told us that we are able to do nothing but bear children. We forgave this since it was the first time. Later it was said about us that we could not discuss politics because the only things we knew anything about were the sounds of machines

and sloshing paint about. We forgave that one too but we were
angry at those who said so. There was a demand for a
Constitution, which, apart from a senate, included also a demand
for eight special representatives, but nothing for the workers.
We forgave this (insult) too, because the generosity of the
Minister for the Colonies saw to the needs of our class. However
we have now reached the point where we cannot forgive the gross
insult received by the working class – an insult which cannot
be forgotten – and the name of Prof. Randon, as author of this
latest insult, will go down in the black book of the enemies of
the people. Prof. Randon told us that Trade Union representation
would degrade the dignity of our Courts. We will add this insult
to the previous ones for the day of reckoning. We now ask, what
could serve the cause of communist propaganda better than
these insults?

Never-ending oppression... Is it not oppression to employ
workers and pay them wages which do not see to their needs
beyond noon of that same day? Is it perhaps not oppression to
leave thousands of workers jobless, to leave them without the
opportunity to earn a living? Is it not oppression to repeal the
rent law at a time when the workers are most in need of it? Is
it not oppression to let children be born weak, through no fault
of their own, children whose only blemish is that of original sin,
and yet they are born into the world weak and anaemic, because
their mothers are undernourished, as a result of poverty? Is it
not oppression to have a clever boy unable to develop his
intelligence due to financial constraints? It is all, all oppression...
and this oppression is generating great propaganda, and it is
doing even more, it has set us going on the road taken by other
nations. It is oppression, and enormous oppression at that, to
get a father to reply – *I haven't any* – when his children beg
him for a mouthful of bread!... It is equally oppressive to let a
father go weeping instead of working... And the government
persists in its oppression by stifling and repealing laws, or
amending them in such a way as to render them useless – laws
which were of benefit to the poor.

Go on, oppress!... Keep on oppressing because you now have
the power to legislate as best suits you. However be careful,

because the people need only that little bit of learning to reach the point that others have reached before. If the people get that little bit of learning they will want to legislate for themselves. We pray to God that what happened elsewhere does not happen here, but our government has chosen the road which other governments have chosen, and the masses will probably have to decide to govern for themselves and in their best interest.

We do not wish to see events taking the same course that was taken in Russia, but we do wish our government to steer another course which feeds the poor, gives drink to the thirsty and clothes the naked.

However this is the road which, far from clothing the naked, strips of every stitch of clothing, and therefore it is necessary that the people "the masses" should learn.

Ugo Parida Izzi

MAY DAY

May Day was publicly and officially celebrated for the first time in Malta in 1926 at the Senglea Labour Club[1] and was presided by the socialist John F. Marks. Leftist activists took part in these celebrations which symbolized the dominant position gained by the left in the Labour movement and the beginning of a socialist orientation of the working masses. The 1st of May was proclaimed as the Socialist League's only feast because it symbolized the adherence of the local working class into a world-wide movement.[2] Accordingly, all socialist militants had to help in every way in the organization of May Day. They were also duty-bound to propagate its significance as a day of struggle for an eight-hour working day and for the emancipation of humanity from class oppression .

Haddiema! Immela l'euuel ta Mejju hia il festa vera tan-nies tax-xoghol tad-dinja collha, data memorabbli ghal haddiem, data li fiha ixxerred id-dinja u din chienet bhal zerrigha, biex f'dan il jum il proletariat b'ghajta uahda tipprotesta fid-dinja collha contra cull ghamil chiefer tat-tiranni li iridu izommu lil poplu ilsir taghhom[3]

While celebrating this day which was considered 'sacred' and given religious attributes by the activists of the working class, the socialist league made great emphasis on the worker's educational aspect [4]. Thus, months before this day, every year, the committee of the League discussed the ways and means in which the 'worker's holy feast' was to be celebrated, and what

---

[1] GHPM., *L'Idea Socialista*, p.13

[2] *Ctieb ir Regolamenti*, ST., p.240

[3] [Workers! The first of May is the true feast of the working-people of all the world, a memorable day for the worker, a day which was spread all over the world, and this was like a seed, so that in this day the proletariat, in one voice, will protest all over the world against every cruel deed coming from the tyrants who want to keep the people enslaved.] S.Pulis, *L'Euuel ta Mejju*, p.5.

[4] *ibid.* pp.2, 5.

was to be published and distributed to the masses on the this occasion. In 1929 the pamphlet *L'Euuel ta Mejju* written by Salvu Pulis was printed by the GH.S.M. in its own printing press. The literature published by the socialist league activists emphasised the internationalist aspect of the struggle of the working people against Capital. It also declared the maltese worker's class solidarity with the struggles of its brethren all over the world.[5] This was most important for the Socialist League which at variance with other maltese labour organizations, boasted of being internationalist and struggled against the provincialism, which it feared could alienate and thus incapacitate the local working masses.[6]

---

[5] ibid. p.5.

[6] ibid., See also the following flysheet, *1 ta Mejju* .

1 TA MEJJU.

Haddiema. F'dan il jum tal 1 ta Mejju jum ta ferh, ghazis, ta mistrieh, ta paci. F'dan il jum haddiema, cullhadd, il haddiema tad-dinja collha jghollu lehenhom u icantau in.ijet ta ferh, innijet ta fratenitá: IMHABBA UNIVERSALI!

L'euuel ta Mejju hia il festa tal haddiema, il festa ta dawc li jghixu f'a.iq ta suied il kalb, mdallma b'duhhan tal ufficini, hia il festa ta dawc li uakt li jinzlu fil minieri isibu ruiehhom mirduma. L'euuel ta Mejju hia il festa tal procession bla tniem ta haddiema mkatta u sofor li jghixu b'biccin hobs mizbugin bi ftit zejt, hia il festa tal ulied il haddiema oppressi, b'uiccom maghlub u morda sfors ittbatija u il giugh, hia il festa tal haddiema li jibcu f'silenziu ta zmien tuil: uakt it-torturi, tax-xoghol!......

Hia il festa taghna li fiha cull haddiem jgholli lehnu ghal avvenir gdid ta Giustizia, ta Libertá, Paci. Hia il festa ta cull bniedem li ihoss li hua bniedem ghandu fiha jieha parti biex ghal li gej il haddiem jaccenista il hacma f'idejh stess, b'hacma chif ghanda teun ghal gid ta culldadd: gh. s-Suffragiu Universali!

L'euuel ta Mejju giet stabilita li gaala besi cull sena mad-dinja collha bhala festa tal Proletariat: fil Congress Socialista Internazionali li chien f'Parigi il-1889.

Haddiema Maltin, immela ahna ucoll ghandna niccelebrau din il festa li fiha nuru lil min irid jghucchisna li ahna ucoll nesistu, li ahna ucoll ghal li gej irridu il jedd, dac il jedd li hu taghna!

Viva L'euuel ta Mejju il festa tal haddiema tad-dinja collha!......

L'GHAKDA SOCIALISTA MALTIJA

Tip. L'Internazionali." MALTA.

1st of May

Workers. Today, the 1st of May, is a cherished day of joy, of rest, of peace. On this day, workers, everybody, the workers of the world, all raise their voices in song, singing hymns of joy, hymns of fraternity: UNIVERSAL LOVE!

The 1st of May is the feast of the workers, the feast of those who live in an atmosphere of sadness, darkened by the smoke of offices, it is the feast of those who descend into the mines and find themselves buried there. The 1st of May is the feast of an endless procession of workers, pale and wearing tattered clothes, who live on bread lightly dipped in oil, it is the feast of the sons and daughters of the workers, oppressed, haggard and sick from suffering and hunger, it is the feast of the workers who eat in silence and for long as they endure the torture of hard work...!

It is our feast, when every worker raises his voice for a new future of Justice, of Freedom, Peace. It is the feast of every human being who feels he is a human being, and everyone should take part in it so that, one day, the worker will acquire the reins of power as should be for the benefit of all: for universal suffrage.

It was established that the 1st of May should be celebrated every year, throughout the world, as the feast of the proletariat: this was at the Congress of the Socialist International held in Paris in 1889.

Workers of Malta, all of us therefore should celebrate this feast, and while doing so show those who would oppress us that we too exist, that we too, in years to come, want our right, a right that is ours!

Long live the 1st of May, the feast of the workers all over the world...!

THE MALTESE SOCIALIST LEAGUE.

(Printed at the *Tipografia L'Internazionali* - Malta)

il cotra

LEHEN IL HADDIEM MALTI

Direttur: Giuse Orlando
Asst. Direttur: Salvu Pulis
Amministratur : L. Darmanin

Direz: 143, Str. Britannica il Belt
Amministrazjoni :—
88 Strada Due Porte, l'Isla

Dan fl folju johrog cull nhar ta Hamis
L'abbonament hua la Id. cull 3 xhar hlas
hil kuddiem. Barra minn Malta la.7d

Is-Sitt Sena   28 ta April 1932   244

L'EUUEL TA MEJJU.
JUM LI MA JINTESA KATT.

Fil hin li id-Dinja colla chienet kegħda tisma il cant u il ferħ tal ħaddiema taħha. Fil hin illi ix-xgħażah ħaddiema tad-Dinja chienu colla kakoċċa uaħda mitlufu fil briju tal imħabba bejniethom, geuua Malta dan il Jum tal 1930 chien xhaba seuda għal ħaddiema taħha.

Chien il Jum li fieh ħarget il Pastorali taz-zeuġ Iskħijet, li gie imuiddeb bi dnub meijet dac il ħaddiem li imur jivvota għal Partit tigħu.

Chien l'euuel colp ufficiali sabiex icun mekrud il Partit tal Ħaddiema. Uara bdeu il priedchi, bdeu ma jintgħataux assoluzionijet, bdeu ma ibircux sachemm fl'aħħar uaslu fil minacci lil casini Distrettuali li għandom il ħaddiema Maltin imxerda fil Gżira colla.

Izda anche għal chemm l'dac il jum għaziz għal ħaddiema chien mgħoti dac il colp, il ħaddiema chienu intakpħu xorta uaħda fit-Teatru S. Giorg ta Bormla, u għamlu il testa li chienu ippreparau. Chien lejliet l'elezioni u ħatt ma sata jaħrab dac id-dmir imkaddes li ma icomplix igħein il butu għat-trick tad-daul li lejħa chien ked imexxihom.

Għaddeu sentein l'actar tual minn dac il Jum tal 1930. Għaddeu sentein ta jasar l'actar chiefer għal ħaddiema, immexxija minn Crown Colony Government ta l'acbar killa. Giet il Cummissioni Reali, sar taklib mill akua, beda jtifaccia il bnazzi li ked narau fuk ix-xefak tal Ċ ira li nittamau li jibka riesak actar lejn il ghaziz pajji us. Il maltempata quasi għaddiet għal collox u uasle biex tcun ucoll minn cullhatt maħfura,

billi il bxora li'dina il maltempata għamlet ma chienitx hlief ta gid għal poplu collu, għalliex dan li stess poplu seijer igaudi, floc isofri, il conseguenza li spiċċat minn artna il lingua li chienet kegħda izzommna irsiera taht chicca.

Illum irgiajna quasi quasi ninsabu fli stess posizioni li conna sentein ilu. Lejliet l'elezionijet, u għalchem uieħed deijem jittama il paci biex trakkad ftit-mill glieda

kelila li għoda sejra contra tagħna, dina i paci donna ma hi sef tasal katt. Donnu hem xi ħagia li għoda izzomma il bgħod minn dan il poplu nisrani u tuaijeb, Irridu incomplu nittamau ftit ieħor aħna tal Partit tal Ħaddiema li lesti sabiex naffrontau l'elezionijet taht qualunque circostanzi, izda ma nixtiekux li l'għodu icun jista juaħħal fina fi din il paci ma gicts fuk artna imħabba għamilna.

Ahna ucoll nixtieku narsu il paci. Anzi din il paci nixtieku narsuha minn kalb cullħatt, mingħajr ma tcun minn ħatt furzata, mingħajr ma tcun mgħamula contra ix-xeuka ta ħatt.

Nistħaijel li xi ħatt jistaksi bħal isus : "Il ghalx allura għadu ma tbiddilx l'atteggiament ta l'oħrain bhal ma tbiddel tagħna ?"

Għal-lum ankas għal din il'mistoksija ma irridu inuiegbu. Irridu inzommu ruħna hielsa mill iċchem scusa ta htija li jkilighu fukna anche għal izgħar chelma.

(Icompli fil pagina 2)

SECRET DISPATCHES

ACTIVITIES OF MR. MATT. GILES

MATTHIAS GILES Age 54, married, British born subject, Occupation: Trade Union Official, Address: 57, Lower Union Street, Bristol. Local Secretary of the Workers' Union which is affiliated to the National Federation of General Workers with James O'Grady M.P. Secretary. W. Thorne, M.P., and C. Duncan, M.P. are also connected with this Federation which is perhaps the soundest Labour Federation and consists mostly of unskilled labour. Giles first came to our notice in November 1919 as a result of enquiries made by the Colonial Secretary at Gibraltar, where he was engaged in "organising labour" in the Dockyard and elsewhere. At the time of the enquiry he was described by the Colonial Secretary as a very sound man but it was stated there were rumours that he tried to tamper with the troops on the Rock. He subsequently returned to the U.K. and in 1920 again went to Gibraltar and Malta for the purpose of visiting Trade Union Branches on instructions from the Executive of the Workers Union, Golders Green Road, London. He returned to this country again and early in 1921 made a further journey, to Gibraltar and Malta to visit branches of the Workers' Union there, and also proceeded to Port Said under Executive instructions to transfer a local Workers' Union to the Workers' Union.

During his visit to Malta in 1920, Giles organised the Workers' Union in three Branches:-

Branch No. 1 Dockyard Employees
Branch No. 2 Military Employees (Civilians).
Branch No. 3 Private Employees.

After he left Malta, a central chamber of labour, known as the "Camera del Lavoro" was established. The Committee of this Chamber is formed partly by members from the Committees of the three Branches of the Workers' Union, and partly by persons entirely outside the Union. Its object is to defend the interests of local Labour in the politics of the Island. The "Camera del Lavoro" is not affiliated with the Workers' Union.

Giles obtained considerable support during his stay in Malta, and large numbers joined the three Branches of the Union which he formed. In his public speeches, and his interviews with the Naval and Military Authorities and members of the Government, he adopted a tone of considerable moderation. The following curious facts connected with his visit, however, lead to the assumption that this attitude of moderation was adopted as a cover to his real aims.

1. At a private meeting of the "Imperial Government Workers' Union", (a purely local union which has been in existence for several years) held during the early part of Giles' visit, in the Summer of 1920, Giles, in the course of his address, made the following declarations: "We are out to destroy Governments and to instal Workers in their

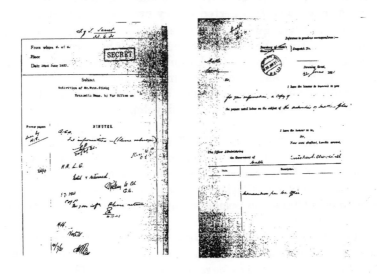

First two pages of Secret Dispatch about the revolutionary activities of Matthew Giles.

place". This statement created such consternation amongst his hearers that he immediately adopted a more moderate tone.

2. Soon after his arrival in Malta, Giles selected three of the worst agitators in the Island as his particular friends; namely, *Michael Angelo BORG, Giacinto TUA* and *William ARENA*. All three men were in financial straits, but, shortly after their acquaintance with Giles, they became well supplied with money.

Soon after Giles's departure from Malta, a formidable campaign against the Workers' Union was launched by the Church. Several Clerical writers took up the subject at length in the Press, and pointed out the anti-Catholic and extreme principles contained in the statute of the Union. His Grace the Archbishop requested Cardinal Bourne to send an eloquent and well qualified priest to Malta to combat the Socialist tendencies which were being inculcated by the Workers' Union. Father Planter, an English Jesuit, arrived in Malta in January and held several meetings. He exerted a very great influence upon his hearers, but he died suddenly after he had been in the Island but a short time. The efforts of the Church have resulted in a serious loss of support to the Union, and a large number of the members have ceased to pay their subscriptions.

Simultaneous to this entrance of Church influence in the Workers' Union, there is the development of a Catholic Organisation, founded by Father Plater, which has been named the "Unione Leoniana". The Church declared the aim of this Union to be the destruction of the growing hatred between Capital and Labour and a closer bond of friendship and co-operation between all classes of society. A large number of workmen's Clubs and Societies have declared their adherence to this Union.

The supporters of Matthew Giles view with consternation the growing ascendency of the Church amongst the members of the Workers' Union and they have been instructed by Giles to make every effort to counteract it by propaganda.

Giles arrived at Alexandria on March 5th 1921 and proceeded to Port Said on the 7th where he was met at the station by

a delegation of the Syndicate of Workmen. Soon after arrival
he had a protracted interview with Dr. Skouphopoulos – President of the "Syndicat Ouvrier International de l'Isthme de
Suez", and a well-known Labour agitator in the Canal zone. But
at this period it was reported that his visit called for no particular comment, his activities confining themselves to his osten-
sible object of linking up the local Workers' Syndicate to the
Workers' Union in England, and his contracts being only those
connected with this body. He had of necessity to be in constant
touch with Dr. Skouphopoulos, in view of the latter's position
as President of the Suez Canal Workers' Syndicate, but it is unfortunate, taking into consideration Skouphopoulos' well-known
revolutionary and anti-British attitude.

As far as could be ascertained Giles's speeches have all been
on comparatively moderate lines with the exception of the usual
invectives against Capitalists. It is curious, however, that the
strike of the Anglo-Egyptian Oilfield Refineries at Suez should
have taken out shortly after Matt Giles's visit to that place.

On the whole it is thought that Giles has not had the complete success he hoped for in Egypt. Although he has managed
to affiliate, in a manner, the Suez Canal Workers' Syndicate to
the Workers' Union, there is still some disagreement over the
payment to be made to the latter union, and several smaller com-
panies have not yet joined the union.

One reason perhaps, of his non-success, is his complete ignorance of oriental mentality and the fact that natives cannot
understand and appreciate Western methods – especially
Western Socialist methods. He confessed as much to an infor-
mant adding that he was surprised at their lack of initiative
and progress.

The success or the non-success of his mission to Egypt,
however, can only be proved in the light of future economic happenings there.

From Egypt, Giles returned to Malta early in May 1921, where
he proposed to remain for about seven weeks. Since his return
he has been very little in the public eye and has addressed only
one insignificant meeting. This is probably due to the many differences in the ranks of the Labour Party, which have arisen

during his absence and which, no doubt, he is now endeavouring quietly to remove.

In addition to the "Workers Dreadnought", which has for some
time been regularly distributed amongst the workers of the
Dockyard, a considerable quantity of other communist literature
has made its appearance. This consists of pamphlets printed,
for the most part, in Manchester and the United States. This
literature is passed from hand to hand amongst the Dockyard
workers with such secrecy that it has not been possible to ascertain the source from which it emanates. This literature, on the
whole, has not had much effect upon the workmen. Their secrecy
regarding it, and their reluctance to allow any of it to pass out
of their hands, is due to their fear that it may find its way into
the hands of their priest and thereby bring upon them the anger
of the Church.

Matthew Giles is reported to have brought a large quantity
of literature with him, but it is not yet known whether this is
of an extreme or moderate character. If any increase of communist literature should be noticed during his stay here, it may
be regarded as emanating from him.

Secret Dispatch exposing the connection between the Sedition Trial and the Language Question

M A L T A,   THE PALACE - VALLETTA.

BEIRUT.   12th June, 1933.

Sir,

I have the honour to refer to my despatch No. 109 of to-day's date, in which I transmit to you five documents concerned with the difficulties experienced by certain persons charged with offences under "The Prevention of Seditious Propaganda Ordinance, 1932" in finding counsel to appear for them before the Courts who were prepared to plead in Maltese. Among this correspondence is a communication from the Chairman and Secretary of the Constitutional Party, and in this connexion I enclose for your information copy of a minute, dated the 26th May, addressed to me by my Legal Adviser.

2.   I am afraid that the minute of the Head of the Ministry which forms Enclosure V to my open despatch partakes of the nature of special pleading and that the reasons given to him by Doctors Harding, Magri and Camilleri for not pleading in Maltese are, to say the least of it, disingenuous. There is no doubt whatever that the great majority of the advocates at present practising in Malta are determined to maintain the supremacy of Italian and to resist the use of Maltese in the Courts for political reasons not connected with the interests of their clients. As things are at present it is likely to take some considerable time before there are available sufficient
willing to plead in Maltese
counsel/to make it possible to implement fully the letter and

spirit

The Right Honourable

Sir PHILIP CUNLIFFE-LISTER, G.B.E.,

&c.,   &c.,   &c.

spirit of the Constitution regarding the use of Maltese in
the Courts of Malta.

I am becoming more and more persuaded that it is
the position still assigned to Italian in the legal system of
Malta - a position which has now become almost an anachronism -
which gives the propagandists in favour of Italian in Malta
their raison d'être and keeps the language controversy alive.
Should it ever become possible to re-affirm the principle
communicated in Mr. Chamberlain's despatch No.39 of the 15th
March, 1899, and subsequently departed from, I believe that the
language question in Malta would very quickly find a permanent,
satisfactory and logical solution.

I have the honour to be,

Sir,

Your most obedient,
humble servant,

(Sd). DAVID G. M. CAMPBELL.

GOVERNOR.

Dispatch No. 60, of 3rd April, 1933.

This Dispatch reveals to what extent the British Authorities had been closely monitoring the Leftist activists in Malta.

MALTA.

No. 60

THE PALACE - VALLETTA.

3rd April, 1933.

Sir,

     In compliance with the request of Mr. Gino Muscat Azzopardi I have the honour to forward the enclosed letter which he has addressed to you on the subject of a search by the Police in his house and offices pursuant to a warrant issued by me under "The Prevention of Seditious Propaganda Ordinance, 1932".

     I have the honour to be,

       Sir,

       Your most obedient,
            humble servant,

(SO. DAVID G. M. CAMPBELL.

GOVERNOR.

The Right Honourable
   Sir PHILIP CUNLIFF-LISTER, G.B.E.,
     &c., &c., &c.

M A L T A.   THE PALACE - VALLETTA.

SECRET.   3rd April, 1933.

Sir,

With reference to my despatch No.60 of to-day's
date, I have the honour to state that acting on information
in the possession of the Defence Security Officer on the
subject of Communistic activities in Malta, I issued Warrants
on the 18th March for searching the houses of nine persons.
The papers and correspondence seized are now being
examined.

2.   Mr. Gino Vincent Assopardi is one of the persons
whose house and offices have been searched and although no
incriminating papers have been found in his case I am of
opinion that in view of what is stated in the accompanying
copies of reports by the Commissioner of Police and the
Defence Security Officer the search in his case was fully
justified.

                    I have the honour to be,
                         Sir,
                    Your most obedient,
                            humble servant,

                         (SD. DAVID G.M. CAMPBELL.

                              GOVERNOR.

The Right Honourable
    Sir PHILIP CUNLIFFE-LISTER, G.B.E.,
        &c.,   &c.,   &c.

COPY.   ENCLOSURE I.

GINO MUSCAT AZZOPARDI, was known to be in touch
with the members of the local Communist organisation. When
the Soviet Trade Commissar, visited Malta in 1931, GINO
MUSCAT AZZOPARDI, was in close touch with him.

GINO MUSCAT AZZOPARDI was a paying member of the
clandestine circulating library consisting of Subversive
Literature, which were seized from the premises of CAROULO
CARABOTT at No.21, Strada Coopicuan, Zeitun.

I suggest reference for further information to
the Defence Security Officer.

30.3.33.

ENCLOSURE II.

COPY.

From a security point of view the main object of the raids was to unearth a Communist organisation (having its Headquarters in the Dockyard) which we know existed but of which we had little actionable evidence.

It was thought that the activities of this organisation were "pink" as opposed to "red", but having regard to the fact that Malta is a Fortress and the majority of its people illiterate there was danger of the movement growing to proportions when it might prove a menace in time of trouble.

As a generalisation it may be said that Communist propaganda is usually started mildly and if unchecked gradually becomes more subversive.

The indications in Malta for the past few months tend to show that this is the case here and that having been unchecked the local Communists are becoming bolder. Articles have appeared in the local press of a "redder" tinge than heretofore and in one or two cases these have been stated by the Police Legal Adviser and/or the Treasury Counsel to actionable under the "Prevention of Seditious Propaganda Ordinance, 1932".

The literature, etc., seized has justified the carrying out of the raids and proved that a definite subversive organisation does exist. The police are now going through all the documents and I understand that there appears to be in most cases sufficient grounds for prosecution under the abovementioned Ordinance.

As far as Gino Muscat Azzopardi is concerned, this gentleman came to our notice when Pozdneff a Russian Trade Commissar visited Malta in September, 1931.

He associates with members of the local Communist organisation.

The raid on the house of Carmelo Carabott, Secretary and Librarian of the local Communist organisation has produced records which show that Azzopardi was a subscriber to this library and from records it can be proved that some of Carabott's literature was delivered to him.

The fact that nothing was found in Azzopardi's house when it was raided indicates, in my opinion, not that he is innocent of Communist activities but that he was either cleverer or more fortunate than his confrères.

Malta. 30th March, 1933.

A CONFRONTATION

The "Viva Calles!" Incident

La vibrata protesta
di S. E. Il Vescovo di Gozo
contro le manifestazioni anticlericali
de_l Stricklandiani

Riceviamo e pubblichiamo con piacere la seguente vibrata protesta di S. E. Mons D. Michele Gonzi D.D., Vescovo di Gozo, contro le sacrileghe manifestazioni stricklandiane di mercoledì scorso—protesta contenuta nella seguente lettera che S. E. Rev.ma ha in 'irizzato al nostro Diocesano in data del 14 c. m. : —

Pal. zo Vescovile
Gozo.

Eccellenza Reverendissima,
I tristi fatti successi a Malta nel pomeriggio di Mercoledì scorso mi hanno profondamente addolorato il cuore di Vescovo e di Maltese.
Come ben dice l'Ill.mo e Rev.mo Vicario Generale di V. E. nella sua Circolare del 13 del corrente mese, mai si sarebbe creduto che dei Maltesi dovessero giungere a bestemmiare Cristo e la sua Santa Religione e ad inneggiare ad un Nerone moderno conosciuto meglio col nome di Calles! Sono state queste delle aberrazioni, che hanno fatto sanguinare il cuore a tutti i buoni, a tutti quelli che amano la Religione nonché il decoro della patria nostra stata sempre per il passato baluardo del Cattolicismo contro ogni sorta di propaganda anticattolica e antireligiosa aperta o subdola: e le bestemmie di Mercoledì scorso sono state delle discrepanse e delle dissonanze in anta armonia. Del resto ogni luce ha la sua ombra e l'ombra per sè stessa mette in rilievo gli splendori della luce. Infatti non può non tornare di grandissima consolazione al nostro cuore di Vescovi il coro di disapprovazione e di protesta, che si sollevò unanime dai giornali e dal labbro di migliaia di buoni nella diocesi di V. E. e in questa mia. Possa il Signore aver pietà di tanti sciagurati e aprire gli occhi a tanti miseri, che han veramente perduto il ben dell'intelletto.
Ho inoltre appreso da fonti autentiche che anche la persona di V. E. è stata gravemente oltraggiata da persone incoscienti, rifiuto delle galere, disonore del popolo nostro buono e religioso nella sua grande generalità. E tutto q to ol aggio a V. E. er la ol

In July 1928, the Compact Government was preparing to review the government's expenses for the current year. For the compactists the Catholic Church was yet another part of a force which resisted this particular fiscal plan.[1] In fact, before the Senate was due to discuss the issue, the compactists published and distributed literature in which they criticized the two clerical representatives (of the senate) - believed to be going to vote against the Government's bill - and called them anti-reformists.[2] On the day the bill was to be discussed a compactist crowd gathered in the main streets of Valletta to protest against the Senate.[3] The crowd walked down all Strada Reale through its side-streets until it reached the Archbishop's Palace. Here anti-clerical slogans were heard.[4] Some were heard insulting the Archbishop *"Abbasso L-Arcisqofu l-kleru!"* [Down with the Archbishop and the Clergy!] and others *"Viva Calles!", "Abbasso Kristu Re!"*

[Long Live Calles! Down with Christ the King!]. Other prominent activists were heard shouting *"Viva l-Messiku!"*. [Long live Mexico!][5] This anti-clerical outburst - which revealed the extent to which the Compact supporters were frustrated by the Church Authorities' anti-reformist stand - was immediately condemned by the Archbishop.[6] In a circular issued by the Archbishop, the latter described the demonstration as anti-religious and blasphemous. According to this circular the main aim of the demonstration was to overthrow Catholicism and create class-hatred. Following the issue of this circular the Senate protested formally against this demonstration.[7] Protest from all popular, religious associations and bandclubs ensued and a wave of anti-compactist propaganda commenced.[8] The Archbishop ordered that reparation be made in all churches in Malta and Gozo for what he considered blasphemous incidents.[9] Along with this circular

...le , .iere, «onci. de. ,»opo, no». .o bu - no e religioso nella sua grande generalità. E tutto questo oltraggio a V. E. per la sola ragione che i Rev.mi Rappresentanti del nostro Clero in Senato avevano quel dopo-pranzo votato secondo le proprie convinzioni. I quali Rappresentanti insieme ad altri ri-spettabilissimi membri del Clero sono stati fatti oggetto di non minore oltraggio nelle pubbliche piazze e nelle vie e perfino dentro l'Aula del più nobile ed alto Consesso na-zionale e ciò non per la prima volta nel breve spazio di poche settimane.

Contro questi fatti sacrileghi, contro que-ste violenze, frutto naturale di una propa-ganda a base di stampati tendenti a denigra-re certe classi della popolazione compreso il Clero ed a seminare tra le masse principii sovversivi ed odio di classe, protesto in no-me della Divinità bestemmiata, della su-prema Autorità Ecclesiastica diocesana vili-pesa, in nome del Clero di ontesta diocesi nonché di questa mia, insultato anch'esso sen-za alcuna ragione da gitanti maltesi or son due settimane. (*) Protesto con tutta l'ener-gia e con tutta la fierezza del carattere epi-scopale, di cui sono investito, dinanzi al Clero e al Popolo delle diocesi di Malta e Gozo, dinanzi a tutte le autorità politiche, amministrative e giudiziarie, nella speranza che queste autorità non macchereranno di cer-care di reprimere questi fatti deplorevoli, che disonorano la patria nostra, e ad impedi-re che simili disordini oramai troppo fre-quenti abbiano a ripetersi. E' sacra ed in-violabile l'ante ità costituita, sacra ed invio-labile la dignità e la civiltà di un popolo, che è sempre susce' ibile di perfezione, pur-ché lo vogliano i dirigenti.

Con questi sentimenti e con tali auguri nel cuore mi è grato raffermarmi

Dall'Eccellenza Vostra Rev.ma
Aff.mo Confratello in Cristo
(Fto.) † Michele, Vescovo di Gozo.

A Sua Eccellenza Rev ma
Mons. Don Mauro Caruana O.S.B.
Arcivescovo Vescovo di Malta.

(*) S. E. Reverendissima allude evidente-mente ai partecipanti della nota gita di pro-paganda organizzata da Stricklandiani.

N. d. R.

which condemned the demonstration, the Archbishop
instituted the Gunta tal-Istampa t-Tajba [Council for the
Honest Press] with the aim of combatting anti-Catholic
literature. This was the birth of Lehen is-Sewwa - the voice
of the Catholic Church in Malta. [10]

[1] Oral Testimony given by Carmelo Zammit.

[2] *Min ma jivvutax il ligi tan Nefka hua xewwiex tal poplu u igib l'Anarkija fil Paijis* Malta 2/8/1928.

[3] ibid.

[4] Oral testimony given by Carmelo Zammit.

[5] ibid.; *Eccessi anti religjuzi u blasfemi*, Malta 23/7/1928.

[6] ibid.

[7] *Il Governo di fronte al clero*, Malta 2/8/1928.

[8] Malta 23/7/1928.

[9] *Eccessi anti religjuzi u blasfemi*, Malta 23/7/1928.

[10] see the first issue of Lehen is-Sewwa, 1/9/1928.

(Illustration "La Vibrata Protesta..." is taken from Malta 17 Luglio, 1928.)

The Pentecoste Incident

The social tensions created by class antagonism took on an aggressive turn with physical violence spilling onto the streets. As the compact in government vigorously aspired to put forward basic secular reforms within the limits imposed by the 1921 constitution, the opposing anti-reformist movement led by the Catholic Church posed powerful opposition.

On the morning of the 8 June 1930, which according to the Catholic calendar was the feast of the Pentecost (Whit Sunday), the Archbishop was celebrating high mass at St John Co-Cathedral, Valletta. As he began to deliver his sermon in Italian, some sixty compact supporters agitated left the church.[1] Amongst the latter, were Geraldu Ebejer, Carmelo Ritchie and Toni Darmanin, who protested vehemently against the Archbishop's use of Italian in front of a Maltese congregation.[2]

Meanwhile an agitated crowd gathered in front of the Co-Cathedral. On one side, compact supporters assembled. These were led by leftist activists and known members of the Socialist League.[3] Red flags appeared among the rallying. On the other side of the gathering, enthusiastic supporters of the Partito Nazionalista and members of religious organizations led by activists of the Catholic Action Movement retorted by insulting the compactists and acclaiming the church and the Archbishop. Herbert Ganado, an Nationalist activist and later a leading politician, witnessed this experience:

Several of us men and youth in St John Co-Cathedral, led by canons, made for the main door to prevent the crowd from entering. The Archbishop continued delivering the homily. By the time the function was over two crowds had gathered; one in favour the other against the Archbishop.[4]

Inside the Co-Cathedral panic ensued and Revd Antonio Bonnici ordered that the doors of the cathedral be closed. This created greater tension [5] and immediately a counter order was given.[6] After a while the police force arrived on the spot[7] and dispersed the crowd. On appearance of the police the compactists began singing the Red Flag Anthem, waving the red flag[8] and red handkerchiefs.[9] Insults against Catholic Action militants and priests, and the singing of socialist slogans and songs could be heard coming from the compactist crowd[10] in Sda Reale and Sda S. Giovanni.[11]

At the same time a group of compactists ran after an Italian journalist who found refuge in a nearby pharmacy in Sda Reale.[12] The compactists challenged the proprietor of the pharmacy to oust the Italian journalist.[13] Following this incident this Italian journalist by the name of Pancrazio had to leave the island immediately.[14] Within the Co-cathedral the police Superintendent suggested to the Archbishop to leave the church from by back door.[15] However the Archbishop refused as he felt that this would undermine his dignity.[16] Meanwhile the mounted police went up the cathedral's parvis and charged on the compactist crowd.[17]

Amongst the compactists Censu Taliana and Toni Darmanin were said to have agitated the crowd.[18] Carmelo Ciantar, a Socialist League activist was heard shouting anti-clerical and anti-fascist slogans.[19] He also challenged the police to put him under arrest.[20] As the Archbishop was coming out of the Co-Cathedral, Ciantar made an obscene gesture and was immediately put under arrest.[21] Ebejer, insulted a woman who was shouting slogans in favour of the church, by saying: Which religion are you talking about?[22] He also went on to physically attack catholic activists and struck Alfredo Attard who was praising the Archbishop while insulting the Compactists.[23]

The socialist Nestu Laiviera, another prominent member of the GHSM, led the crowd in nearby Sda Reale. As the Archbishop was approaching his carriage which was traditionally drawn by members of the Catholic Action Movement, insults were hurled at the Archbishop for having approved meagre raise in the salary of dockyard workers.[24]

Geraldu Ebejer, Carmelo Ritchie, Censu Taliana, Toni Darmanin, Lazzru Xuereb, Carmelo Ciantar and Constantin Micallef (*Ta Fazolu*) were immediately put under arrest.[25] They were later charged for having, on the 8th of June 1930, trooped in a crowd of more than ten persons, with the aim of breaking the public order. They were also charged of having insulted and ridiculed his grace the Archbishop of Malta and of resisting police officers and passing insults at public officers whose duty it was to maintain public order.[26]

The trial that ensued was to make history. It was the first one to be conducted in Maltese. After several appearances in court, and a handful of controversial happenings and appeals, the final sentence was pronounced on 19th May 1931. Of the accused Geraldu Ebejer was sentenced to a month's imprisonment while Carmelo Ritchie got a two months term. Toni Darmanin, Censu Taliana and Lazzru Xuereb were each sentenced to fifteen days imprisonment. Constantino Micallef was acquitted.[27]

However, some time later, Lord Strickland managed to obtain pardon for these activists. This pardon was heavily criticized by a section of the local press and the Governor was accused of being politically biased.[28]

---

[1] "The Pentecost Jury", *Malta Chronicle and Imperial Services Gazette*, 21st May, 1931.

[2] Ganado, Herbert, *Rajt Malta Tinbidel*, vol 1, p.420.

[3] Arge, "Socialismu", *Il Poplu*, 7/8/1931.

[4] Ganado, Herbert, *Rajt Malta Tinbidel*, vol 1, pp.420-1.

[5] *ibid.* Also oral testimony given by Carmelo Zammit.

[6] "The Pentecost Sunday Jury - First criminal trial in Maltese", *Malta Chronicle and Imperial Services Gazette*, 21st May, 1931.

[7] *ibid.*

[8] "Grajja ta Gheid il Hamsin", *Il Poplu*, 11/7/1930]

[9] Oral testimony given by Tommy Ritchie.

[10] "Grajja ta Gheid il Hamsin", Il Poplu, 11/7/1930

[11] *ibid.*

[12] "The Pentecost Sunday", *Malta Chronicle and Imperial Services Gazette*, 21st May, 1931.

[13] *ibid.*

[14] *Il Cotra*, 28/5/1931.

[15] Ganado, Herbert, *Rajt Malta Tinbidel*, vol 1, p.421.

[16] *ibid.* Also oral testimony given by Carmelo Carabott.

[17] "Li Stampa Stricklandiana u l Pulizija", *Il Poplu*, 30/4/1930.

[18] "Grajja ta Gheid il Hamsin", *Il Poplu*, 14/7/1930

[19] *ibid.*

[20] "Is Sentenza contra il Ponestanti ta nhar l Gheid il Hamsin", *Il Progress*, 7/7/1930.

[21] *ibid.*

[22] *ibid.*

[23] *ibid.*

[24] *ibid.*

[25] *Mid-Day Views*, 27th August, 1930.

[26] *ibid.*

[27] "Sebgha Patriotti", *Id Dehen*, 20/6/31.

[28] Pesci, G., "Il Mahfra ta lic-cundannati", *Il Poplu*, 2/6/1931.

The Pastoral Letter of 1st May 1930

La Parola Dei Due Vescovi

Riportiamo integralmente il testo dell'importantissima pastorale dei due Vescovi letta ieri in tutte le Chiese parrochiali di Malta e Gozo e accolta con la massima soddisfazione e deferenza dall'immensa maggioranza dei fedeli delle due Isole:

DOM MAURO CARUANA O.S.B.

Arcivescovo Vescovo Di Malta

e

Mons. MICHELE GONZI

Vescovo di Gozo

Venerabili fratelli e figli carissimi in Gesù Cristo,

Siamo alla vigilia delle elezioni politiche. L'eccitazione degli animi è già viva come mai per l'addietro, e i buoni aspettano tutti, molto giustamente, da Noi, posti dallo Spirito Santo a reggere queste due diocesi, eminentemente cattoliche, una parola, che sia loro di conforto e di luce in questi momenti di ansia e di confusione.

La Chiesa non a mai preteso di disciplinare gli interessi puramente politici, ai quali deve provvedere lo Stato; ma quando si tratta di tutelare i tesori religiosi e morali del popolo; quando gli interessi della Religione sono minacciati; quando la gerarchia della Chiesa è disprezzata ed è manomessa la sua autorità; quando in una parola la politica si accosata all'altare e l'ordine pubblico corre rischio di essere sovvertito, allora la Chiesa ha il diritto e il dovere di intervenire e di dire a tutti, re e popoli, governanti e sudditi, la verità, e additare a chi di dovere, senza guardare in faccia a nessuno e a costo di tutti i propri obblighi. Che se tali pericoli hanno la loro origine da parte di coloro che hanno in mano le redini del Governo, o si temono da parte di coloro, che si preparano ad insediarsi nel governo, allora la Chiesa si rivolge ai fedeli suoi sudditi, dal cui suffragio dipende il benessere religioso e sociale, e ad essi, ricorda l'obbligo a loro devoluto di avvantaggiare e di difendere la Religione. Questa è stata sempre la condotta della Chiesa attraverso il lungo volgere dei secoli; ne così comportandosi, la Chiesa ha fatto o fa della politica, come insinuano i suoi detrattori. La Chiesa fa una unica politica: quella della salute delle anime, della gloria di Dio, dell'onore suo; e questa non è politica, ma è pura religione, come ebbe a dire il regnante Pontefice Pio XI nella sua allocuzione ai pellegrini maltesi e gozitani nell'Agosto scorso. E la nostra condotta pastorale è stata sempre ispirata ai principii cattolici sopra enunciati. Non abbiamo mai ostacolato l'attività prettamente politica di alcun partito politico; non abbiamo cercato mai di avvantaggiarne alcuno a danno degli altri, finché i diversi partiti politici locali si contennero entro i limiti della politica, senza invadere il campo religioso. Senonché le circostanze attuali nel paese sono molto diverse. Chi ha attentamente e spassionatamente esaminato le controversie sorte tra le Autorità Ecclesiastiche e il Governo locale, nonché le cause, che le hanno determinate, ha dovuto assolutamente ammettere - checché se ne dica in contrario - che le questioni in parola riguardano la Religione. E non lo ha dichiarato con parole esplicite lo stesso S. Padre nella Lettera spedita a Noi, Vescovi di queste Isole, per mezzo di S. E. il Cardinale Gasparri in data del 30 Giugno u.p.? Il

Papa, ben conoscendo dai Rapporti di Monsignor Delegato Apostolico la gravità della situazione, Ci confortava ed esortava Noi Vescovi a continuare colla dovuta fermezza non disgiunta dalla necessaria prudenza, nella linea di condotta da Noi fino allora tenuta contro l'atteggiamento di alcune Autorità dell'attuale Ministero, e vi parlava di attività nociva quanto mai alla Religione ed alle più sacre tradizioni cattoliche della patria nostra da parte di queste Autorità, invitando tutti i fedeli di queste Isole a intensificare le loro preghiere onde ottenere dal cielo il miglioramento della penosa situazione, ed invocando la cessazione di tanto danno da parte delle Autorità responsabili. Queste però nonché sottomettersi alla paterna parola del Papa ed obbedire - come conveniva a chi si trovava al governo di un popolo eminentemente cattolico - osarono discutere l'augusta parola del Vicario di Gesù Cristo e ribellarvisi con gravissimo scandalo dei buoni e pregiudizio alla disciplina cattolica del nostro buon popolo. Noi pastori di queste diocesi non abbiamo taciuto davanti a questo atteggiamento delle Autorità del Ministero e di coloro che le assecondarono; abbiamo alzato la nostra voce di protesta contro tanto scandalo con tutta l'énergia e con tutta la fierezza del carattere episcopale, da cui la Provvidenza Divina ci ha voluto investire, invitando allo stesso tempo i responsabili e i loro seguaci al ravvedimento e ad una sottomissione figliale al Padre di tutti i Cattolici. Ma le nostre parole caddero su terreno sterile. Abbiamo ripetuto le nostre offerte di pace, ma abbiamo esatto ancora segni pubblici ed evidenti di resipiscenza. Nè abbiamo potuto fare altrimenti: lo scandalo era pubblico, e la riparazione quindi doveva essere pubblica; l'ordine pubblicamente violato doveva pubblicamente reintegrarsi. La pace non poteva dissociarsi dalla giustizia. E lo stato di ribellione alla parola del Papa durava e dura ancora - Ci rincresce doverlo constatale - da parte del Governo di Malta Cattolica.

Di fronte a così penose stato di cose, nei tristi momenti che attraversiamo, non abbiamo potuto non indirizzare a voi venerabili fratelli e figli dilettissimi, che vi gloriate come della vostra maggior gloria di appartenere alla Chiesa Cattolica, questa Nostra Lettera per confermare i buoni, per iscuotere gli indolenti, per illuminare gli erranti, per ammonire chi agisce con mala fede. La nostra parola è stata finora è sara ancora libera e franca, quale si addice a chi ha ricevuto da Dio la missione di illuminare le anime. Non piacerà forse a tutti; la colpa però non è nostra. È sempre grave cosa il dire una verità amara; ma quanto meglio una verità che contrista, di una menzogna che inganna. Gli inganni passano e lasciano rovine; la verità rimane e salva. E Noi ve l'abbiam detto sempre la verita e ve la diremo a costo di tutto e per il dovere, che abbiamo, di illuminarvi, e per il bene, che vi portiamo. Nulla varrà a chiuderCi la bocca.

Nelle attuali circostanze l'uso del diritto del voto diviene un sacro dovere di coscienza e di responsabilità. È obligo imprescindibile di ciascuno di voi di non rimanere spettatori indifferenti ed inermi di fronte a quanto con animo profondamente addolorato constatiamo accadere in mezzo a noi. Non bastano i lamenti e le proteste; occorre agire. Da buoni figli della Chiesa irrigata dal sudore della fronte dell'Apostolo Paolo dovete coi fatti mostrare al mondo, che s'interessa delle nostre penose condizioni, che non facilmente si vilipendono le nostre secolari tradizioni cattoliche e che i sacrileghi conati per alienarvi dallo spirito e dalla disciplina cattolica non sono valsi ad altro che a vieppiù avvicinarvi ed unirvi a chi ha da Dio ricevuto il mandato di esservi guida e salute, per essere sempre coi vostri Vescovi, col Papa, nella Chiesa, con Cristo. Mostrate coi fatti che, quando si tratta della fedeltà alla Santa Sede e al Papa di Roma, voi siete, come i padri vostri invurnerabili. È per voi questo un obbligo assai grave di coscienza, su cui per nessuna ragione al mondo potete chiudere gli occhi e passarvi sopra. Chi col suo voto aiuta correnti e uomini dai quali non può sicuramente sperare una strenua difesa degli interessi della Religione ed un cosciente lavoro cristiano nello stato e nella società, non agisce da Cattolico.

E per venire al concreto e non lasciare nei vostri animi alcuna titubanza sappiate che come cattolici: 1) non potete senza commettere peccato grave, votare per Lord Strickland e per i suoi candidati, nonché per tutti quelli, anche di altri partiti, che lo hanno pel passato assecondato ed appoggiato nella sua lotta contro i diritti e la disciplina della Chiesa, o che intendono assecondarlo ed appoggiarlo nelle prossime elezioni; 2) a più forte ragione non potete presentarvi come candidati nelle liste elettorali proposte da Lord Stickland o da altri partiti, che comunque intendono appoggiarlo nelle prossime elezioni; 3) siete inoltre gravemente tenuti in coscienza, nelle presenti circostanze, di prendere parte alle elezioni e di votare per quelle persone, che, per il loro passato diportamento, offrono maggior garanzia, tanto per il benessere religioso, quanto per il benessere sociale.

Onde impedire poi gli abusi nell'amministrazione e nella ricezione dei Sacramenti, facciamo ricordare ai nostri sacerdoti che e loro severamente proibito di amministrare i Sacramenti agli ostinati, che rifiutano di ottemperare a queste nostre istruzioni. Fa proprio pena il vedere dei cattolici, rei di pubblica e grave violazione della disciplina cattolica, continuare liberamente ad accostarsi ai Sacramenti con grande ammirazione dei buoni. È tempo che i responsabili compiano con fermezza e senza rispetti umani il loro dovere, se non vogliono attirarsi l'ira del Giudice Divino.

Vi esortiamo ancora, e lo facciamo con tutto il Nostro cuore paterno, a tenere la calma, ad osservare l'ordine e la tranquillità pubblica e non ricorrere mai alla violenza o alla provocazione.

Raccomandiamo a tutti, clero e popolo, d'innalzare insieme con Noi fervide preghiere a Dio e ai Santi Protettori di queste diocesi, affidando nelle loro mani le sorti della patria nostra. A questo fine ordiniamo che dalla ricezione della presente fino a nuovi ordini, in tutte le chiese, prima della Benedizione Sacramentale, si recitino cinque *Pater*, *Ave* e *Gloria*, seguite dal *Veni Creator* colle Orazioni: "*Deus qui corda*", "*Concede*" e "*Deus, qui multitudinem gentium*".

Vogliamo in fine che la presente nostra Lettera Pastorale venga in tutte le Chiese pubblicata ai fedeli Giovedì prossimo, il primo giorno del mese dedicato alla Vergine Maria, Madre nostra. E, nella fiducia che il Buon Pastore, per l'intercessione della Santissima Madre Sua e nostra, vorrà degnarsi esaudire le nostre preghiere e concederci la pace religiosa e sociale, che sospiriamo, vi benediciamo nel nome del Padre e del Figliuolo e dello Spirito Santo.

Dato il dì 27 Aprile 1930.

† MAURO O.S.B. Arcivescovo Vescovo di Malta

† MICHELE Vescovo di Gozo

Can. P. Buttigieg
Can. M.A. Scerri Cancellieri

The Bishops' Pastoral Letter of June 1932

Circolare No. 293
DOM MAURO CARUANA, O.S.B.,
Arcivescovo Vescovo di Malta
e
MONS. MICHELE GONZI
Vescovo di Gozo

Venerabili Fratelli e Figli carissimi in Gesù Cristo,

Siamo lieti di annunziarvi che Lord Strickland riconoscendo il male che ha fatto alla Religione e alle più sacre tradizioni cattoliche di Malta in questi ultimi anni col suo atteggiamento verso la Chiesa e la Sua Autorità, ne ha dichiarato al Santo Padre il suo sincero rincrescimento, domandandone umilmente e senza riserva perdono, come si può vedere dalla lettera di scusa dello stesso Lord Strickland a Sua Santità il Papa, qui annessa.

Il Santo Padre sempre pronto ad accogliere i figli erranti, che si manifestano sinceramente pentiti, ne ha accettato queste scuse.

Il sopravvenire di questo nuovo fatto toglie motivo di perdurare alla Pastorale da Noi pubblicata il 1 Maggio 1930, segnatamente per quello que riguarda la persona di Lord Strickland.

A Noi Vescovi di queste Diocesi Maltesi non rimane quindi, per conscienzioso debito del nostro Ministero Pastorale, se non ricordare a tutti i fedeli affidati alle nostre cure l'obligo di coscienza che, come a tutti i cattolici, loro incombe di dare il loro voto soltanto a quei candidati, che diano sufficienti garanzie che, per quanto da loro dipende, saranno rispettati e

tutelati gl' interessi religiosi del cattolico popolo maltese, interessi che sono la base di ogni civile e sociale prosperità.

Nella speranza che abbia ora a regnare tra tutti la pace da Noi tanto sospirata, impartiamo a tutti la nostra Pastorale Benedizione.

Dato oggi, 3 Giugno 1932, Festa del Sacralissimo Cuore di Gesù.

✝ Mauro O.S.B.
Arcivescovo Vescoco di Malta,
✝ Michele,
Vescoco di Gozo.

Can. P. Buttigieg,
Cancelliere

Copia della lettera di scusa di Lord Strickland a Sua Santità

[Copia] Villa Bologna. Malta 28. 5. 1932.

/ A Lord Strickland Conte della Catena rincresce sinceramente, che in dibattimenti nel Parlamento Inglese e nel Parlamento Maltese, ed in altre occasioni, nel defendersi contro i suoi oppositori politici, abbia urtato contro la Chiesa e la Sua Autorità, ed usato parole che devono essere ritirate, e che di fatto ritira, ed umilmente e senza riserva ne domanda perdono.

Gli è a cuore poi di dichiarare enfaticamente, che durante tutta la sua vita fu sempre suo fermo proposito di essere figlio fedele della Santa Chiesa nel cui grembo è suo desiderio di rimanere sempre.

(ft.) STRICKLAND DELLA CATENA.

(Extracted from *Malta*, June 1932.)

THE LEGALITIES OF
A CASE

PREVENTION OF
SEDITIOUS PROPAGANDA

IMPORTANT ORDINANCE BY
THE GOVERNOR

A very important Draft Ordinance was issued on Saturday evening whereby provision is made for preventing seditious propaganda and for intercepting all seditious matter imported into Malta and for preventing the distribution thereof.

Defining what seditious matter means, the Ordinance says:

"Seditious matter" means any printed or written matter, signs or visible representations contained in any newspaper, poster, book, letter, parcel or other document and any gramophone record, which are or is likely or may have a tendency, directly or indirectly, whether by inference, suggestion, allusion, metaphor, implication or otherwise:

(a) to seduce any officer, soldier, sailor or airman in the Army or Navy or Air Force of His Majesty from his allegiance, or his duty, or to cause disaffection in these Forces towards His Majesty;

(b) to bring into hatred or contempt or to excite disaffection against the person of His Majesty or the Government and the Constitution of the United Kingdom, or the Constitution of Malta, or of the Government or Constitution of any other British Possession or Protectorate as by law established;

(c) to incite His Majesty's subjects to take up arms against His Majesty's Government or to attempt, otherwise than by lawful means, to compel His Majesty's Government to change its measures or counsels or to obstruct the exercise of its lawful authority;

(d) to raise discontent or disaffection among His Majesty's subjects; or

(e) to promote feelings of ill-will and hostility between different classes or races of such subjects.

PENALTIES

Any person who is guilty of an offence against this Ordinance shall be liable, on conviction, to imprisonment with hard labour for a term not exceeding four years or to a fine not exceeding £500 or to both such imprisonment and fine.

AN ORDINANCE enacted by the Governor of Malta in the exercise of the powers conferred on him by His Majesty's Letters Patent dated, the 14th of April, 1921, constituting the office of Governor and Commander-in-Chief of Malta.

To prohibit the importation, publication, possession and distribution of seditious matter.

WHEREAS in virtue of Section 12 of His Majesty's Letters Patent dated the 14th April 1921, constituting the Office of Governor and Commander-in-Chief of Malta, the Governor may by any Ordinance, to be by him issued, make laws for the peace, order and good Government of Malta, with regard to matters reserved from the Legislature of the Island, by the Malta Constitution Letters Patent, 1921, and therein defined as Reserved Matters;

AND WHEREAS the prevention and repression of seditious propaganda are Reserved Matters as affecting the public safety and defence of the Empire;

AND WHEREAS it is expedient to make provision for preventing seditious propaganda and for intercepting all seditious matter imported into Malta and for preventing the distribution thereof;

Be it therefore enacted as follows:

1. This Ordinance may be cited as "The Prevention of Seditious Propaganda Ordinance, 1932".

2. In this Ordinance:

"Malta" means the Island of Malta and its Dependancies;

"Seditious matter" means any printed or written matter, signs or visible representations contained in any newspaper, poster, book, letter, parcel or other document and any gramophone record, which are or is likely or may have a tendency directly or indirectly, whether by inference, suggestion, allusion, metaphor, implication or otherwise:

(a) to seduce any officer, soldier, sailor or airman in the Army or Navy or Air Force of His Majesty from his allegiance or his duty, or to cause disaffection in these Forces towards His Majesty;

(b) to bring into hatred or contempt or to excite disaffection against the person of His Majesty or the Government and

Constitution of the United Kingdom, or the Constitution of Malta, or of the Government or Constitution of any other British Possession or Protectorate as by law established;

(c) to incite His Majesty's subjects to take up arms against His Majesty's Government or to attempt otherwise than by lawful means to compel His Majesty's Government to change its measures or counsels or to obstruct the exercise of its lawful authority;

(d) to raise discontent or disaffection among His Majesty's subjects; or

(e) to promote feelings of ill-will and hostility between different classes or races of such subjects.

Provided that no such matter, representation or record shall be deemed seditious matter by reason only that it is likely, or may have a tendency, to show that His Majesty or any Government as aforesaid, has been misled or mistaken in his or their measures, or administrative or other action, or to point out errors or defects in, or to incite His Majesty's subjects to attempt by lawful means the alteration of any matter by law established;

"Postal article" means any letter, postcard package, newspaper, printed matter, parcel and every article or thing transmissible by post and shall include a cablegram or radiogram.

3. It shall be lawful for the Governor acting by and with the advice of the Nominated Council, by express Warrant in writing under his hand, to direct that any postal article suspected of containing any seditious matter, shall be intercepted or detained or shall be delivered to any person or persons mentioned in such Warrant to be disposed of or dealt with in such manner as the Governor may direct.

4. Any person authorized by the Governor by express Warrant in writing under his hand may search, open and detain any package, parcel or any other thing imported or brought into Malta whether by land, sea or air which he suspects to contain seditious matter, and may detain, during such search, any person bringing such package, parcel or any other thing into Malta.

5. Where it appears to the Governor that there is reasonable cause to suspect that any seditious matter exists in any building, vessel or place, the Governor may by Warrant in writing empower any Police Officer not below the rank of Superintendent of Police, to enter and if necessary to break into or forcibly enter such building, vessel or place and to search and take possession of any seditious matter which may be found there.

6. Any person who prints, publishes, imports, whether by land, sea, or air, sells or offers for sale, distributes, exhibits or exposes, or without lawful excuse has in his possession any seditious matter, shall be guilty of an offence against this Ordinance.

7. Any person to whom any seditious matter has been delivered without his knowledge or privity shall forthwith deliver to the Commissioner of Police such seditious matter and in default he shall be liable to be convicted of an offence against this Ordinance.

Any person who has complied with the provisions of this article shall not be liable to be convicted of the offence of having in his possession any such seditious matter.

Any person who is guilty of an offence against this Ordinance shall be liable on conviction to imprisonment with hard labour for a term not exceeding four years or to a fine not exceeding £500 or to both such imprisonment and fine.

SENTENCE PRONOUNCED BY THE COURT IN THE CASE THE POLICE vs CARMELO CARABOTT and OTHERS

11 di 14 Agosto, 1933.

LA POLIZIA.
Sotto Ispettore Emmanuele Calleja
vs
Carmelo Carabott ed altri.

LA CORTE,

Sulla imputazione avanzata dalla Polizia contro Carmelo Carabott, John Valvo, Giusè Orlando, Luigi Pulis e Joseph Storace, tradotti in arresto innanzi a questa corte per aver in luoghi diverse a Malta, durante il periodo dal 15-9-32 e il 18-3-33, importato, distribuito ... in violazione alla Ordinanza del 1932 per la prevenzione di propaganda sediziosa.

Viste le note illustrative dell'imputazione presentate dalla Polizia assistita dal P.L. A. German.

Visti i documenti presentate...

Sentiti i testimoni sia quelli prodotti dalla prosecuzione siaquelli dalla difesa;

Sentiti sotto giuramento gli accusati;

Udite le parti;

Altrocchè il valorare, abile e detta difensore l'A. Bartolo, nelle parte preliminare della sua tesi difensiva, assume che il presente giudizio non è alto che un colpo di scena, una manovra, un espediente politico, allo scopo di screditare gli imputati...

E risaputo che su questi giudizi incombe una duplice responsabiltà quello di S.E. il Governatore cui unicamente per la delicata natura delle questioni involute abbia luogo e quella dell' Magistrato che è l'Ordinaria responsabiltà di ogni giudizio. E disposto infatti all'Articolo 5 della Ordinanza citata: "Apparendo al Governatore che vi sia ragionevole motivo di sospettare che materia ... esiste in qualunque edificio, bastimento o luogo, egli potrà, mediante mandato in iscritto, autorizzare qualunque ufficiale di Polizia, non inferiore al grado di soprintendente, di entrare o se necessario di forzare o di entrare forzatamente in qualunque edificio, bastimento o luogo e di perquisire e prendere possesso di qualunque materia sediziosa che vi si possa trovare.

Devesi quindi escludere che S.E. il Governatore nell'adempimento dei suoi doveri a norma della detta disposizione dilegge abbia potuto ordinare le perquisizione e le procedure consenquenziali, senza che avesse esaminato i fatti e visto che almeno prima facie vi era luogo a procedere.

Attesocchè lo stesso difensore attaccò la prosecuzione accusandola di aver agito contro lo spirito della legge inglese col produrre innanzi al tribunale soltanto quei documenti di se altri la cui produzione avrebbe formato prova a favor loro.

Questa accuse non sembra che sia giustificta. Se è vero che non tutti i libri, le carte ecc., elevati dal potere degli imputati furono profatti in giudizio, è ugualmente vero che gli altri furono in parte restituiti e in parte trattenuti e lasciati a disposizione degli imputati.

Attesocchè la difesa, considera la legge fondamentalmente, essenzialmente e caratteristicamente inglese, essendo la stessa amanata dal Governatore in virtù dei poteri suoi straordinari come capo della Diarchia Imperiale, col parere del Consiglio Nominatore e come materia riservata, e invoca che la stessa debba ricevere quella interpretazione... alle idee e ai principii ed alla giurisprudenza inglese su questo punto, giova rillevare...

L'Ordinanza del 1932 per la prevenzione di propaganda sediziosa punisce ancora la provocazione **indiretta**.

Così è punito colui che importi, vendi, distribuisce ecc., qualunque stampato che possa anche indirettamente, tendere a sedurre i membri delle forze di S.M. dalla loro fedeltà, dai loro doveri ed a provocare disaffezione negli stessi verso S. Maestà; Così è ugualmente punito colui che tenga in suo possesso uno scritto che indirettamente possa incitare i sudditi di S.M. a prendere armi contro il Governo o a tentare, altrimenti che per mezzi legali, a costringere il Governo di S.M. a cambiare le sue misure e risoluzioni; così ancora è punito colui che con qualsiasi mezzo provedute dall'Ordinanza possa anche indirettamente provocare malcontento e disaffezione tra i sudditi di S.M. a promuovere sentimenti di ostilità tra le diverse classi o razze di tali sudditi

Ne deriva che uno stampato, uno scritto aventi i caratteri dell'Ordinanza ... non sarebbe incriminabile in Inghilterra come non sarebbe stato in Malta alteriormente all'Ordinanza...

A conferma di ciò basta citare la decisione data da questo tribunale in ... "La Polizia vs Giuseppe Pace ed altri il dì 13 Ottobre 1932..."

Attesocchè risulta dagli accertamenti di fatto: che nel
15/9/32, data dalla promulgazione della Ordinanza per la
prevenzione di propaganda sediziosa, l'GH.S.M. non era
cessata. Essa spiegava impunemente la sua attività. Il 18
Settembre 1932 alcuni degli affiliate, tra i quali gli imputati
Carabott,Valvo, Azzopardi tennero un incontro e fissarono un
altro al 26 dello stesso mese nel quale ultimo incontro
procedettero alla elezione del loro presidente detto D.
Degiorgio.

Che l'Ghakda era regolata da uno statute, ed era diretta al
fine di difondere a Malta e all'estero la dottrina socialista
anorma dei principii socialisti internazionali...

L'affiliato professava di essere Socialista e prometteva di
prestare l'opera sua a favore del movimento Socialista col porre
la sua firma alla dichiarazione che in questi termini: *"Jen li
ghaun ismi...*

Che secondo lo Statuto Cap. IV, verso 1, l'affiliato veniva
chiamato col nome *'Sieheb'* della sua compartecipazione e
cooperazione verso l'edificio della Repubblica Socialista
Internazionale...

Che l'Ghakda agiusta lo Statuto Cap VI, verso 7, accettare
letteratura di idee moderate come pure estreme. Essa aveva
una stamperia. Furono stampate e publicati per cura della
stessa *L'Idea Socialista* nel 1926, Homo *Lill Haddiema* nel
1927, *X'inhua is Socialismu* nel 1928 e *Il Faxxismu* nel 1929.

Che l'Ghakda aveva una libreria. Carabott che ne era il
libraio era incaricato della vendita dei libri. Veniva pubblicata
la lista dei libri... e si dava avviso che gli stessi erano vendibili
presso il libraio; No. 11 Melchiorre Gafà Str., Zeitun. La vendita
dei libri non fu discontinuata dopo l'Ordinanza. Ne fanno prova
i registri elevati dal potere di Carabott...

Che agli affiliati e agli amici dell'Ghakda si davano libri da leggere a casa. In un opposito registro elevato dal potere di Carabott se ne teneva un notamento. Questo registro fornisce la prova che si davano i libri sia prima sia dopo l'Ordinanza; l'ultima registrazione porta le date del 5 Marzo 1933...

Che la stemma dell'Ghakda, gusta risoluzione degli affiliati nella Seduta generale tenuta il 25/3/28, ricordata a pag. 28 del *'Ctieb il minuti'* era la falce e il martello. Nella discussione l'imputato Pulis, aveva proposto l'emenda che attorno la stemma si scrivessero le parole di Marx *"Haddiema tad-digna Nghakkdu"*.

Che nelle seduta che I'Ghakda dovesse affiliata all' I.C.W.P.A. Questa Associazione si era occupata del caso "Sacco e Vanzetti", creando una agitazione allo scopo di ottenere la loro liberazione.

L'Ghakda Socialista Maltija nel fatto si affiliò all'I.C.W.P.A. come risulta dall'"Affiliation Receipts' a mezzo di Carabott riceveva dalla stessa la sua letteratura...

Che l'Ghakda sia prima sia dopo la promulgazione dell'Ordinanza importava, vendeva e distribuiva materia sediziosa...

Che... fu in possesso di pochi libri e di alcuni numeri di giornali, nonchè del ritratto di E. Dimech offerti in vendita dall'Ghakda...

Chi era veramente Dimech lo attesta ... egli fu condannato cinque volte per furto, due volte per vagabondaggio, una volta per omicidio e un altra volta per contraffazione di moneta. Lo attestano ... i suoi scritti che Valvo dice di conservare per lo studio di ortografia...

Extract from the original preserved at the Law Courts in Malta.

8 novembre 1933
Giudice: L'Illmo, R.F. Ganado, LL.D.

La Polizia *versus* Carmelo Carabott ed altri

Appello—Ricorso di Appello—Nullità

L'eccezione di nullità del ricorso di appello per mancanza degli elementi essenziali che deve contenere è sollevabile di ufficio.

Tale eccezione può essere sollevata dalla Corte anche quando è composta di un sol giudice.

La mancanza di uno solo degli elementi del ricorso di appello enumerati dalla legge, sia dei fatti in compendio, come dei motivi di aggravio, nonchè della domanda per la revoca o riforma della sentenza, importa sempre la dichiarazione della nullità del ricorso medesimo.

Non si uniforma al voto della legge l'appellante che nel suo ricorso di appello omette totalmente i fatti o accenna solamente taluni.

La Corte — Visti i ricorsi (1) di Carmelo Carabott, (2) di John Valvo, Giuseppe Orlando, Luigi Azzopardi e Salvatore Pulis, (3) di Joseph Storace, i quali chiedono che la sentenza resa dalla Corte Criminale dei Magistrati di Malta il dì 14 agosto 1933 colla quale si dichiarò constare contro ciascuno degli imputati del reato contro l'Ordinanza del 1932 per la prevenzione di propaganda sediziosa e vennero condannati alle pene ivi indicate, sia da questa Corte revocata;

Vista la detta sentenza della Corte Criminale dei Magistrati di Malta in virtù della quale Carmelo Carabott venne condannato alla pena della prigionia per tre mesi e alla multa di £15; John Valvo alla stessa pena per un mese e alla multa di £10; Giuseppe Orlando alla stessa pena per due mesi e alla multa di £10; Luigi Azzopardi alla stessa pena per due mesi e alla multa di £10; Salvatore Pulis alla multa di £15 e Joseph Storace liberato ai termini dell'articolo 23 delle Leggi Criminali;

Visti gli atti della causa suddetta;

Uditi i difensori degli appellanti e l'Assistente Prosecutore Pubblico sull'eccezione sollevata di ufficio della nullità dei ricorsi presentati dagli appellanti;

Considerando,

Che l'istituto di appello dalle sentenze della Corte Criminale dei Magistrati come Corte di Criminale Giudicatura conosciuto nella nostra legislazione penale (fatta eccezione di alcuni casi

contemplati nell'articolo 235 delle Leggi di Polizia, in cui si
concedeva un appello nello stesso modo e sotto le stesse
condizioni e innanzi la stessa Corte come s'interpone da
qualunque sentenza della Corte della Polizia Giudiziaria in
materia civile), è stato per la prima volta introdotto
coll'Ordinanza XV del 1888 limitatamente però ad alcuni casi,
casi tassativamente indicati nell'articolo 5 pel condannato, e
nell'articolo 2 per l'Avvocato della Corona. Nell'articolo 8 di
detta Ordinanza era provveduto che "il ricorso di appello deve,
a pena di nullità, contenere una succinta narrazione del fatto,
una indicazione del motivo di appello come tale motivo è espresso
in quella Ordinanza, e la domanda per la revoca della decisione
della Corte Inferiore". La detta Ordinanza rimase in vigore fino
l'anno 1900, quando in una legge emendante le nostre leggi
criminali è stato aggiunto un capitolo numerato III e intitolato
"Degli appelli dalla sentenze della Corte della Polizia
Giudiziaria come Corte di Criminale Giudicatura". L'appello
venne esteso pel condannato in modo illimitato, ma non così per
la Prosecuzione che poteva appellarsi in casi determinati; alcune
delle disposizioni dell'Ordinanza XV del 1888 sono state tolte,
altre però sono state emendate; l'articolo intorno al ricorso di
appello (art. 412 ediz. 1901) rimase sostanzialmente lo stesso.
Invero in detto articolo, oggi articolo 118 è provveduto che "il
ricorso oltre le indicazioni comuni agli atti giudiziari dovrà
contenere sotto pena di nullità: 1) i fatti in compendio; 2) i motivi
di appello; 3) la domanda per la revoca o la riforma della
decisione della Corte Inferiore; 4) la firma di un avvocato o
dell'Avvocato della Corona. Da ciò emerge che tanto nell'antica
legge quando in quella che la succedette, e che è attualmente
in vigore, la narrazione dei fatti si richiede − tanto equivalgono
le espressioni "narrazioni dei fatti in succinto nella prima legge,
e "i fatti in compendio" nella legge attuale, ed hanno un
medesimo significato: *"Leges posteriores ad priores pertinent
nisi contrariae sine"*;
     Che l'Ordinanza VIII del 1909 apportò diversi emendamenti
alle Leggi Criminali anche nel capo degli appelli, siccome si sono
estesi i casi in cui si dà appello all'Avvocato della Corona, ma
nessun emendamento è stato fatto alle disposizioni che
riguardavano il ricorso in appello;

Che nell'anno 1913, in seguito a raccomandazioni fatte dietro
la Commissione Reale inviata a Malta nell'anno 1911 il
legislatore apportò diverse modificazioni al Codice di Procedura
Civile (Ordinanza XV del 1913), in special modo riguardo la
nullità comminata dalle leggi antiche alla petizione in appello,
dando la facoltà alla Corte di permettere all'appellante di
enunciare per via di 'Note' le particolarità richieste dalla legge.
Tale disposizione non fu incorporata nelle Leggi Criminali,
sebbene in quello stesso giorno fu promulgata una Ordinanza
emendante le Leggi Criminali (Ord. No. XII del 1913) e si
emendarono alcuni articoli nel capo "Degli Appelli";

Che dal premesso emerge chiara la conseguenza che il
legislatore venne a mantenere in vigor le disposizioni che
comminano la nullità di certi atti quando non riuniscono i
requisiti voluti dalla legge. E non si può dire che la omissione
sia involontaria perché il legislatore dove ha voluto ha dichiarato
espressamente che la mancanza di certi requisiti non importa
nullità come nei casi contemplati nell'articolo 375 delle Leggi
Criminali, in cui è disposto tra altro: "non risulterà alcuna
nullità dall'inosservanza delle disposizioni contenute nei
precedenti paragrafi di quest'articolo". Lo stesso si può dire delle
modificazioni apportate all'atto di accusa per errori od altro che
precedentemente importavano nullità; perché si diede la facoltà
alla Corte di correggerli, ecc. (art. 573 delle dette Leggi);

Che inoltre si desume dall'articolo 427 delle stesse leggi e
giusta il capo "Degli Appelli", che "la legge impone alla Corte
tassativamente l'obbligo di annullare la sentenza della Prima
Corte nel caso di violazione di forme prescritte dalla legge sotto
pena di nullità ad altrimenti sostanziali. Se la legge è quindi
così rigorosa in tali casi occorsi dinanzi la Prima Corte, non può
ritenersi diversamente per forme e per i requisiti sostanziali di
un atto che si presenta dinanzi questa Corte, quando è
comminata la nullità per la inosservanza di uno dei requisiti
di tale atto. Per lo che quando si muove controversia sulla nullità
dell'atto", scrive il Pisanelli (Commentario del Codice di
Procedura Civile. Vol. I, p. 458 Ediz., 1875 Napoli), "per
inosservanza di requisiti, non havvi altro criterio che il testo
espresso dalla legge; devesi oggi indagare quali forme essa

prescrive sotto pena di nullità e se siano state trascurate", e in un'altra linea dice che "le formalità estrinsiche ricevono tutta la loro forza dalle sole autorità della legge, ne la volontà di essa può dai privati o dal Magistrato minimamente alterarsi;.........";

Che le nullità assolute provenienti da una legge motivata dal pubblico interesse, denominate nullità di interesse pubblico, non si possono in alcun modo sanare e quindi l'atto che non riveste tutti gli elementi richiesti dalla legge per la sua validità, e che sono essenziali, non ha esistenza giuridica insin dal suo inizio; Considerando.

Che la nullità di un atto comminata dalla legge deve (e non già può) essere sollevata di ufficio per la ragione che è una legge di ordine pubblico e quindi non lasciata alla volontà di alcuno di potere sanare le omissioni alle sue disposizioni, né alle parti in lite, né al giudicante. Invero, se si dovesse procedere oltre, trascurando la quistione di nullità, si verrebbe a creare altri atti nulli; la nostra legge di procedura all'articolo 113, reso applicabile alle leggi criminali dall'articolo 499, dispone che "Gli atti giudiziari fatti in virtù ed in conseguenza di un atto nullo sono ugualmente nulli". Quindi nella fattispecie tutte le procedure che seguiranno e tutti gli atti che si faranno saranno nulli e di nessun valore giuridico, perché l'atto iniziale, il ricorso, che dà secondo la legge l'autorità a questa Corte a conoscere la causa in grado di appello, essendo viziato, mancando di uno degli estremi che lo renderebbero nullo, non può dare la necessaria giurisdizione a questa Corte di conoscere la causa. Le nostre leggi di Procedura Civile allo articolo 799 indicano i casi in cui si può dare l'eccezione di nullità non è comminata dalla legge, che dalla dizione sembra che richiegga la parte avversa ad opporla, negli altri casi la eccezione è sollavabile di ufficio; e nella pratica quotidiana si hanno diversi casi di nullità della petizione di appello per mancanza di uno degli elementi di casi di incompetenza e di altri, atti, quando la nullità è comminata espressamente dalla legge, che la nullità venne sollevata di ufficio. E questa Corte ha ritenuto che tale eccezione di nullità, essendo di interesse pubblico è sollevabile di ufficio (La Polizia vs. Ernesto Laivieri, 18 ottobre 1930; e Stella Bond vs. Vincenza Ellul, 14 ottobre 1933);

Che l'argomento che si può trarre dall'articolo 800 delle Leggi di Procedura Civile che dispone che l'eccezione data in seconda istanza della nullità della sentenza su cui versasse l'appello non dovrà attendersi ognora che tale sentenza si trovasse sostanzialmente giusta, è che è necessario una disposizione di legge espressa per autorizzare la Corte e non attendere alle eccezioni di nullità; in conseguenza quando tale autorizzazione manca, il Giudice non può, senza erigersi a legislatore e trasandare ai suoi doveri, di non pronunciarsi sulla eccezione di nullità dell'atto, che è suo obbligo di sollevare se non viene sollevata dalla parte avversa;

Considerando,

Che l'essere questa Corte costituita di un sol Giudice e non già di tre Giudici, come è costituita generalmente per certe accuse e non può decidere tutte le eccezioni che si sollevano sull'atto di accusa, non può servire di argomento perché questa Corte, come è costituita in virtù della legge, debba astenersi dal sollevare eccezioni di ufficio, perché essa è investita dei medesimi poteri come se fosse una Corte Collegiale;

Considerando,

Che come è stato costantemente ritenuto, dalla nostra giurisprudenza, la mancanza di uno degli elementi del ricorso sopra indicati sia dei fatti in compendio come dei motivi di aggravio nonchè quello della domanda per la revoca o riforma della sentenza importano sempre la dichiarazione della nullità del ricorso (La Polizia vs. D'Agostino, 5 gennaio 1899; La Polizia vs. Busuttil, 9 ottobre 1899; La Polizia vs. Zahra. 18 agosto 1896; La Polizia vs. Spiteri, 22 settembre 1896; La Polizia vs. Mamo, 10 agosto 1899; La Polizia vs. Galea, 30 settembre 1911; La Polizia vs. Zammit, 27 ottobre 1917: La Polizia vs. Laiviera, 18 ottobre 1930; e Stella Bond vs. Vincenza Ellul, 14 ottobre 1933);

Che in queste due ultime cause si è ritenuto che non si uniformi alla lettera e allo spirito della legge chi omette i fatti in compendio o i motivi di aggravio. Non colla lettera perchè la legge richiedente quegli elementi si riferisce a quello che realmente accade, a narrare i fatti come avvennero, e non a narrarli in modo diverso da quello in cui seguirono; non alla spirito, perché si viene ad eludere il motivo informante da disposizione di dare contezza dei fatti accaduti e dei motivi di aggravio; ed è stato pure ritenuto che non si ottempera neppure al voto della legge il menzionare la imputazione o l'esporre la dichiarazione della convinzione o della liberazione, anche indicando articoli di legge, perché col ciò fare e il tacere dei veri fatti come occorsi oppure del motivo di aggravio è una elusione alla legge comminante la nullità del ricorso;

Considerando

Che gli appellanti allegano che nella pratica non si è mai osservato il preciso disposto di questa legge. A parte la questione che se si è fatto male in altre occasioni non si può da ciò trarre alcun argomento, sta di fatto che, richiamata in qualsiasi modo l'attenzione del giudicante alle omissioni di uno dei requisiti del ricorso, questa Corte ha sempre dichiarato la nullità. Supposto, però, come mera ipotesi, che tale pratica abbia avuto il carattere di uso, può tale uso abrogare la legge scritta? La negativa è la risposta data dalla Corte di Cassazione Francese. Invero un arresto della detta Corte del 25 gennaio 1841 dice: "Attesocchè le contravvenzioni ad una disposizione legislativa non possono essere legittimate dal loro medesimo numero; attesocchè supponendo la esistenza di un uso quasi generale di formare gli atti notarili fuori la presenza dei testimoni e di contentarsi della firma dei testimoni (ciò che sarebbe una vana formalità senza causa e senza utilità), un simile uso in opposizione con una legge formata nell'interesse di un ordine pubblico sarebbe 'un abuso che non deve essere consacrato'; attesocchè se sotto un regime nel quale la consuetudine era legge; l'uso poteva abrogare una legge scritta, non potrebbe essere così in un tempo in cui la legge scritta è ugualmente resa notoria a tutti; attesocchè la Corte di Cassazione il cui dovere è di vegliare all'esatta applicazione delle leggi e di mantenerli non può sanzionare un abuso che la violi apertamente". Alla stregua di tali principii questa Corte non può accettare quanto allegano gli appellanti, che la legge che richiede certe formalità nel ricorso cadde in dissuetudine, perché tale allegazione non è suffragata né dai fatti nè dalla dottrina in proposito;

Considerando.'

Che nella specie non vi è nessuna menzione dei fatti nel ricorso di Carmelo Carabott come richiede la legge; egli nel suo ricorso fa consistere i fatti in compendio nella imputazione di essere stato egli membri prominente del 'Għaqda Maltija', di aver preso parte attiva nelle deliberazioni di detta società, di avere avuto in suo possesso materia sediziosa e di essere stati elevati alcuni libri e documenti. Ciò non soddisfa al voto della legge né alla lettera, né al suo spirito. Invero non si uniforma alla lettera della legge, sia omettendo totalmente i fatti sia accennando alcuni, perché la legge richiedente l'elemento dei fatti in compendio si riferisce a tutto ciò che sia realmente accaduto e risultato a carico e a discarico dell'imputato; si verrebbe pure a violare lo spirito della stessa legge perché mancando di menzionare i fatti o accennando alcuni si viene ad eludere il motivo informante la disposizione di dare contezza dei fatti accaduti. Non si ottempera neppure al voto della legge con menzionare l'imputazione e descriverla, perché ciò sarebbe una elusione alla legge, che richiede la narrazione dei fatti non in tutti i loro dettagli, ma compendiati (Appello Criminale, La Polizia vs. Laivieri, 18 ottobre 1930 e Bond vs. Ellul, 14 ottobre 1933 e altri casi decisi recentemente). La parola "compendio", usata dal legislatore, nel suo significato etimologico significa discorso che raccoglie in poco il valore intrinseco del discorso più lungo; ed è tra le composizioni più difficile e più proficuo, se buono, ed ha lo stesso significato della parola 'in succinto' (Tommaseo e Bellini, voci 'Compendio' e 'Succinto', Ediz. U.T.E.T.).

Ed è massima di legge che le parole si debbano prendere nel loro senso ordinario. In conseguenza i fatti in compendio o in succinto, come richiedeva pure la legge anteriore, richiedono sempre la narrazione degli stessi;

Considerando,

Che nel ricorso di John Valvo, Giuseppe Orlando, Luigi Azzopardi e Salvatore Pulis, vi è riportata la sentenza della Prima Corte del reato di cui vennero convinti e della pena irrogata, si menzionò il rigetto delle eccezioni e vengono dati i motivi di aggravio. Nessuna menzione è stata fatta dei fatti e non si possono desumere gli stessi da altre parti del ricorso perché non ve ne sono. I motivi di aggravio non possono supplire al difetto dei fatti in compendio per la ragione che sono dei requisiti diversi richiesti dal legislatore per la validità del ricorso:

Che vi è anche l'omissione dei fatti nel ricorso di Storace non contenendo lo stesso che l'imputazione addotta contro di lui, la condanna della Corte e i motivi di aggravio, e perciò anche tale ricorso non è valido;

Per tali motivi,

Dichiara irrito, nullo e di nessun effetto giuridico (1) il ricorso di appello di Carmelo Carabott del 19 agosto 1933; (2) il ricorso di appello presentato lo stesso giorno 19 agosto 1933 di John Valvo, Giuseppe Orlando, Luigi Azzopardi e Salvatore Pulis; (3) il ricorso di appello di Joseph Storace del 19 agosto 1933.

THE

SEDITION CASE

OFFICIAL CORRESPONDENCE

BETWEEN

JOSEPH ORLANDO SMITH

AND

THE IMPERIAL AUTHOR

JUSTICE!

An Appeal to British opinion

Under the pretext of having contravened the Sedition Ordinance, my political adversaries succeeded in persuading Sir David Campbell, Malta's present Governor, to sign a warrant for the search of my office and the house of my father who was ill in bed.

I was also arrested and dragged before the Law Courts, where, accompanied by some books confiscated from my library of about 2,000 volumes, I have undergone a severe and hard trial of not less than 35 sittings and the Magistrate condemned me to two months imprisonment and a fine of £10.

I immediately lodged an appeal for what is considered to be one of the most unjust persecutions that ever happened to a Britisher under the liberal British Flag, but, under the pretext that my lawyer's application for appeal was not sufficiently detailed, the Judge dismissed my appeal and I was sent to gaol.

As soon as released I tried to obtain justice for what I had been subjected to in this political persecution, in which my reputation and business have suffered enormously.

Encouraged by the speech of Sir John Simon, made in Glasgow on the 25th February, 1934, I addressed several communications to the Governor, with requests that same be transmitted to the Rt. Hon. The Secretary of State for the Colonies, in the hope that Sir John Simon's speech, re British Justice and Liberties, applied also to all Britishers, including those living in Malta, but, the present Governor, is apparently determined to stick to the erroneous advice he was given, when he warranted the raids and my arrest.

However, my British feelings and admiration for the fair play of the majority of English administrators, still gives me confidence to see my case redressed, and it is in this genuine expectation that I decided to publish in this form all the official correspondence between me and the Imperial Authorities trusting that my efforts to be justly treated will not be vain.

Joseph Orlando Smith

Source: *The sedition case: Official correspondence between Joseph Orlando Smith and the Imperial Authorities*

THE SEDITION CASE: COMMENTS FROM THE INTERNATIONAL PRESS

The "EVENING STANDARD" writes as follows:

"Seditious Matter" surprise for Lord Passfield.

Lord Passfield (Sidney Webb) expressed surprise today when an "Evening Standard" representative called his attention to the fact that some of his works were taken by the police in raids on the homes of four Maltese who were sent to prison yesterday for being in possession of "seditious matter".

Other books by Karl Marx, Tolstoy, and Bernard Shaw were mentioned – Lord Passfield said.

"I had no idea that any of my writings were being regarded as seditious and cannot conceive which of my books, in the list of about 30, could possibly be so described.

"It may be, of course, that something about Malta to which I put my name when I was Secretary for the Colonies has been so construed by lawyers, but I do not understand why it should be".

The "NEWS CHRONICLE" makes the following remarks:

"Seditious matter"

There may be more behind the case in which three Maltese were sent to prison yesterday and a number of others fined for being in possession of "seditious matter". But if the seditious matter really consisted as the reports suggest, of works of Marx, Tolstoy, Shaw and Sidney Webb, there would seem to be something wrong with the law, either in Malta or in England. Assuming the possession of the works of these authors to be "seditious" a considerable minority of our population ought apparently to be in prison.

The same paper publishes the following:
"All my Books seditious" says Shaw.

Asked to comment on the Malta trial result, Mr. Bernard Shaw said to "News Chronicle":
"All my Books are seditious. So are the others mentioned in the case.

But they ought to prosecute me and not the unfortunate men who buy the books.

They are not to know what is in them."

"THE LITERARY GUIDE"

Malta, December, 1933

A Blow to Fascism

Dramatic events have occurred in Malta since we called attention to the sedition case in our October issue. The Governor has suspended the Constitution, dismissed the Ministry, and remitted the sentences of the six sedition prisoners. Reuter's dispatch containing this last information states that the Governor exercised his prerogative of mercy becasue "A technical flaw" in the notice of appeal prevented a rehearing. The real facts concerning this "technical flaw" are of a gravely disquieting nature. The notices were prepared by experienced solicitors and were in the customary form. It had not occurred to the prosecution that there was any ground of objection, the difficulty being raised of his own motion by the presiding judge in the appeal court. The latter quoted a case decided in 1902, but this case had been ignored by him during his twelve years on the bench. It is extremely significant that in the course of the next few days this judge rejected no less than seven notices of appeal on the same ground, which proves that the form adopted was that in ordinary use.

It will be remembered that one of the prisoners was described by the magistrate as an anti-Fascist, this being apparently conclusive of his guilt, and it is notorious that the late Government of Malta was under the patronage of Mussolini. Recent events are a warning to Fascist conspiritors that their pernicious system will not easily establish itself on British territory. The love of liberty, though sadly weakened in these latter days, is not yet dead. We are interested to hear that a typewritten copy of our October article was sent to the presiding judge and read in court...

Scathing comment by Italian Paper
On "So-Called British Liberty"

Il Mattino, one of the leading papers in Italy, published a telegram from London, dated August 17th, stating that "the English papers have given great prominence" to the trial, and reproducing in full the substance of their reports. It also includes Bernard Shaw's comments, which it qualifies as "ironical". The telegram which is published under the heading "Maltese condemned because they read Tolstoy and Shaw" concludes with the following trenchant comment:

"This trial is generally regarded as an illuminating example of how elastic and relative is the so-called liberty which is enjoyed in British countries".

Bibliography

Bibliography

◆ **PRIMARY UNPUBLISHED SOURCES**

The Palace Archives, Valletta.

Secret dispatch from S.S.C. W. Churchill to Gov. Plumer, 'Concerning M.A. Borg, G. Tua and W. Arena. Requests to be informed immediately in the event of departure of, from Malta.' 17 May 1921.

Secret dispatch from S.S.C. W. Churchill to Gov. Plumer, 'Transmits Memo. by War Office on Archives of Mr. Matt. Giles', 22 June 1921.

Secret dispatch from S.S.C. W. Churchill to Gov. Plumer, 'Matthew Giles and the Labour Movement in Malta; Transmit copy of a War Office Letter', 28 June 1921.

Dispatch from S.S.C. Lord Passfield to Gov. John Du Cane, 14 January 1931.

Dispatch no. 60, Gov. D. Campbell to S.S.C. Cuncliffe Lister, Enclosure I and II, 'Concerning search by the Police in the house of G. Muscat Azzopardi', 3 April 1933.

Law Courts Archives.

Sedition Trial, April - August 1933.

◆ **ORAL TESTIMONIES**

Carabott, Carmelo, interviewed by the author, 7 January 1985.

Ritchie, Tom, interviewed by the author, 23 March 1986.

Zammit, Carmelo, interviewed by the author, 21 March 1986.

◆ **PUBLISHED REPORTS**

Malta Royal Commission 1931, Minutes of Evidence, H.M.S.O. London, 1932.

Humphreys, J.H, Report on the first general elections of general members of the Senate and of members of the Legislative Assmbly

Malta Government Gazette, Supplement LIV, 11 November 1921.

◆ **PUBLISHED PAMPHLETS AND FLY-SHEETS BY THE *GHAKDA SOCIALISTA (PROLETARIA) MALTIA***

Anon., *L'idea Socialista*, (Ghakda Proletaria Maltia, John Bull Press, Malta 1926).

Anon., *X'Inhu is-Socialismu*, (Ghakda Socialista Maltia, Tip. L'Internazionali, Malta 1928).

Homo, *Lill Haddiema*, (Ghakda Socialista Maltia, Tip. L'Internazionali, Malta 1927).

Pulis, Salvu, *Il Faxxismu*, (Ghakda Socialista Maltia, Tip. L'Internazionali, Malta 1929).

Il Bandiera Hamra, (Ghakda Socialista Maltia, Tip. L'Internazionali, Malta 1928).

L'Euuel ta Mejju, (Ghakda Socialista Maltia, Tip. L'Internazionali, Malta 1928).

◆ PRIMARY PRINTED SOURCES

Amery, L.C., *My Political Life, War and Peace 1914 - 1929*, vol. 2, (Hutchinson, London 1953).

Anon. *La Questione Nazionale e Linguistica Dopo il Colpo di Stato del 2 Novembre 1933*, (Malta 1935).

Azzopardi, Wigi, *Il-Fakar*, (Stamperija Lombardi, Malta 1927).

Bellanti, P.F., *L-Enciclica 'Rerum Novarum' migjuba bil-Malti*, (Malta 1921).

Bonnici, Giuse, *L-Istorja tal-Partit tal-Haddiema*, (Kummissjoni Propaganda, Malta 1931).

Borg, Mikielang, *Karambola - Gabra ta' Ittri u Artikli f'Gurnali li wara li jolqtu Lilna jduru kollha fuq il-Kumpanija Filodrammatika Maltija 'L'Indipendenza'*, (Stamperija Nazzionali, Malta 1938).

Ciano, Count Galeazzo, *Diario 1937 - 38*, (Capelli, Bologna 1948).

Degiorgio Duminku, *Il-Guerra tad-Dinja jeu l-Ikbar Omicidju Kollettiv*, (Lux Press, Malta 1939).

Ellul Mercer, Guzè, *Leli ta' Haz-Zghir*, 2e., (Associated News, Malta 1983).

Ganado, Herbert, *Rajt Malta Tinbidel, (1900-1933)*, vol. 1., (Interprint, Malta 1977).

Mamo, Juann, *Ulied in Nanna Venut fl'Amerca*, (Tip. Ant. Ellul, Malta 1930).

Orlando, Giuse, *Pamphlet tal Partit tal Haddiema*, (Partit tal Haddiema, Malta 1929).

Orlando, Giuse, *Liz-Zghazagh*, (Dar tal Partit tal Haddiema, L'Isla, Malta 1929).

Orlando, Giuse, *The Sedition Case, Official correspondence between J. Orlando Smith and the Imperial Authorities*, (Malta, 1934).

Paris, P., O.P., *"Rerum Novarum" fuk il condizionijiet tan-Nies tax-xoghol*, (Malta, 1930).

Programm Elettorali tal 'Partit tal-Haddiema', (Tip. Nazionale, Malta 1921).

Swinton, R. Viscount, *I Remember*, (Hutchinson and Co. Ltd., London 1946).

Tonna Barthet, A., *Iz-Zerriegha l-Hazina*, (Malta, 1927).

◆ **MALTESE NEWSPAPERS**

II Berka, 1933.

II Bandiera tal Maltin, 1911.

II Cotra, 1926 - 1933.

Daily Malta Chronicle, 1921 - 1928.

Id Dawl, 1931.

Id Dehen, 1931.

II Fkir Malti, 1923.

Il Ggant, 1929.

II Habib, 1926 - 1928.

Il Hmar, 1920, 1926 - 1928.

II Hmara, 1929 - 1931.

Internazionali, 1929.

II Kuddiem! Lehen il Haddiem Imcasbar, 1933.

Labour Opinion, 1922 - 1926.

Lehen is-Sewwa, 1929.

Malta, 1928.

The Malta Chronicle and Imperial Services Gazette, 1932 - 33

Malta Government Gazette, 1921, 1927, 1929, 1939.

Malta Herald, 1923.

Malta Labour Leader, 1924.

Malta tal Maltin, 1922 - 1924.

Militia Christi, 1928, 1933.

In Nazzjon - folju Nazzjonalista, 1926.

Il Patriott Malti, 1927.

II Poplu, 1929.

II Progress, 1921 - 1924.

The Times of Malta, 1926.

It-Torca, 1981.

L'Unjoni Maltija, 1919 - 1920.

Il Veru Patriott Malti, 1927.

◆ FOREIGN NEWSPAPERS.

Daily Worker, 15 August 1933.

The Times, 14 August 1933.

The Scotsman, 13 February 1932.

◆ SECONDARY PRINTED SOURCES.

Anon., *Il-Qawmien tal-Haddiem Malti*, vol.1, (Malta 1971).

Azzopardi, Geraldu, *Ghejdut Manwel Dimech - Kitba u Hsibijiet ta' Dimech*, (Union Press, Malta 1978).

Azzopardi, Geraldu, *Meta il-Malti Ghadab: Is-7 ta' Gunju 1919 - 60 Sena Wara*, (Partit tal-Haddiema, Malta, 1979).

Azzopardi, Geraldu, *Il-Fundaturi tal-Partit tal-Haddiema*, (S.K.S., Malta 1984).

Azzopardi, Mario, 'Socio-Realisti Madwar Ellul Mercer', *Mis-Sillabu*, vol.1, no.8, (PEG Publications, Malta 1984).

Bartolo, Paul, *X'kien Gara Sew fis-Sette Giugno*, (K.K.M., Malta 1979).

Carocci, G., *La Politica Estera dell'Italia Fascista 1925 - 1928*, (Editori Laterza, Bari 1969).

Cassells, G., *Mussolini's Early Diplomacy*, (Princeton University Press, Princeton, New Jersey 1970).

Carroni, Umberto, 'Crisi Ideale e Transizione al Socialismo', *Critica Marxista*, (Editori Riuniti 1976).

Engels, F. 'Principles of Communism', Marx, K. and Engels, F., *Selected Works*, vol.I, (Progress Publishers, Moscow, 1977).

Fenech, Dominic, *The Making of Archbishop Gonzi*, (Union Press, Malta 1976).

Frendo, Henry, *Party Politics in a Fortress Colony. The Maltese Experience.* (Midsea Books, Malta 1979).

Gramsci, Antonio, *Selections from the Prison Notebooks*, (Lawrence and Wishart, London 1976).

Klugmann, James, *History of the Communist Party of Great Britain - Formation and Early Years 1919-1924*, vol.1, (Lawrence and Wishart, London 1976).

Klugmann, James, *History of the Communist Party of Great Britain; The General Strike 1925-1926*, vol.2, (Lawrence and Wishart, London 1976).

Koster, Adrianus, *Prelates and Politicians in Malta*, (Vijfhuizen, Rotterdam 1981).

Laferla, A.V., *British Malta (1872-1921)*, vol.2, (Aquilina & Co. Publishers, Malta 1977).

Mc Leod, G.H., *Religion and the People of Western Europe 1789 - 1970*, (Oxford University Press, Oxford 1981).

Mifsud Bonnici, R., *Dizzjunarju Bijo-Bibliografiku Nazzjonali*, (Department of Information, Malta 1960).

Niekerk, A.E., van, *Populism and Political Development in Latin America*, (Rotterdam University Press, Rotterdam 1974).

Pelling, Henry, *A Short History of the Labour Party*, (McMillan Press, Cambridge 1978).

Pelling, Henry, *The Origins of the Labour Party*, 1880-1900, (Oxford, 1965).

Poggi, G., *Calvinism and the Capitalist State - Max Weber's Protestant Ethic*, (MacMillan Press, London 1983).

Ryle, Martin J., 'International Red Aid and Comintern Strategy,1922-1926', *International Review of Social History*, vol.15, (1970).

Sant, C., 'Protestant Maltese Bible Translation; The Gospel of St. Mark ', *Journal of Maltese Studies*, no. 13, (University Press, Malta 1979).

Schiavone, Michael J., *L-elezzjonijiet f'Malta 1849-1981*, (Pubblikazzjoni Bugelli, Malta 1987).

Spadolini, Giovanni, *L'Opposizione Cattolica, da Porta Pia al' 98*, (Oscar Mondadori, le Monnier, Firenze 1972).

Zammit, Edward L., *A Colonial Inheritance*, (University Press, Malta 1984).

◆ **SECONDARY UNPUBLISHED SOURCES.**

Borg, Reno, *The Maltese Worker, 1919 - 1939*, (Unpublished B.A. Hons. Dissertation, University of Malta 1975).

Mintoff, Dionisju, *Journalism in Malta - An Account and Appreciation*, (Unpublished M.A. Dissertation, University of Malta 1971).

Index

Index